IN THE SPIRIT OF
WILLIAM JAMES

IN THE SPIRIT

OF

WILLIAM JAMES

BY

RALPH BARTON PERRY

PROFESSOR OF PHILOSOPHY
HARVARD UNIVERSITY

Published for Indiana University.

GREENWOOD PRESS, PUBLISHERS
WESTPORT, CONNECTICUT

Library of Congress Cataloging in Publication Data

Perry, Ralph Barton, 1876-1957.
In the spirit of William James.

   Reprint of the ed. published by Yale University
Press, New Haven, issued in series: Powell
lectures on philosophy at Indiana University, 2d
ser.
   Includes index.
   1. James, William, 1842-1910. I. Title.
II. Series: Indiana. University. Powell
lectures on philosophy: Second ser.
B945.J24P38 1979   191   78-31937
ISBN 0-313-20715-1

Reprinted with the permission of Yale University Press.

Reprinted in 1979 by Greenwood Press, Inc.
51 Riverside Avenue, Westport, CT 06880

Printed in the United States of America

10 9 8 7 6 5 4 3 2 1

THE
MAHLON POWELL FOUNDATION

MAHLON POWELL—1842–1928

WABASH, INDIANA

Extract from the last Will and Testament of Mahlon Powell:

Having entertained a desire for many years to assist in the cause of a higher education for the young men and women of our state and nation, and to that end provide a fund to be held in trust for the same, and to select a proper school or university where the same would continue in perpetuity, I will, devise and bequeath all of the real and personal property that I possess and of which I die seized to the Trustees of Indiana University, Bloomington, Indiana, to be held by them and their successors in office forever, the *Income* only to be used and applied in the support and maintenance of a *Chair* in *Philosophy* in said institution, and to be dedicated and forever known as "The Mahlon Powell Professorship in Philosophy" of said University.

In accordance with the provisions of this bequest, the Trustees of Indiana University have established a Chair in Philosophy on The Mahlon Powell Foundation. Each year a Visiting Professor will be invited to fill this Chair. The second lecturer on The Mahlon Powell Foundation is Professor Ralph Barton Perry of Harvard University.

WILLIAM LOWE BRYAN

To
E.P.A.

PREFACE

THE present volume consists, with some slight additions, of lectures delivered at Indiana University in January, 1937, on The Mahlon Powell Foundation. To the memory of the founder, to the authorities of the University, and to my colleagues of the Department of Philosophy of that University, I desire to express my gratitude. I acknowledge my obligations to Little, Brown and Company for their permission to draw freely from my larger work on *The Thought and Character of William James;* to Mrs. Josiah Royce for her generous assistance in the compilation of biographical material relating to her late husband; and to Rosamond Chapman for her loyal and skillful coöperation in the preparation of my manuscript. The title of these lectures indicates my endeavor to be at one and the same time true to William James and to myself.

RALPH BARTON PERRY

Cambridge, Mass., February 13, 1938.

CONTENTS

xii   William James

IN THE SPIRIT OF
WILLIAM JAMES

CHAPTER I

TWO AMERICAN PHILOSOPHERS

IN the summer of 1849 the elder Henry
James wrote as follows to his friend Emerson:

My wife and I are obliged—so numerous has
waxed our family—to enlarge our house in town,
and get a country house for the summer. These
things look expensive and temporary to us, be-
sides being an additional care; and so, looking
upon our four stout boys, who have no play-
room within doors, and import shocking bad
manners from the street, with much pity, we
gravely ponder whether it would not be better
to go abroad for a few years with them, allow-
ing them to absorb French and German and get
a better sensuous education than they are likely
to get here.[1]

The eldest of these "four stout boys" was William James, then living with his parents on
West Fourteenth Street, New York City. Although only seven years of age, he had al-

1. R. B. Perry, *The Thought and Character of William
James* (1935), I, 59.

ready spent a year and a half in Europe. His
family enjoyed comfortable means, good social position, and all the advantages of a met-
ropolitan residence. His father, the friend of
Emerson and Thoreau, numbered among his
familiar associates not only the Concord circle
but other distinguished men of letters at home
and abroad. William's education, begun under the tutelage of "educative ladies," was
thereafter entrusted to a perpetually changing series of tutors and private schools. Although his formal instruction was broken and
unsystematic, his experience was steadily cu-
mulative in its effects of urbanity, culture,
and social adaptation.

During this same summer of 1849 a little
family party of three was crossing the American continent, having set out from eastern
Iowa to find their fortunes in California. The
head of this family was a certain Josiah Royce
—an Englishman from Rutlandshire who in
childhood had migrated with his parents to
Dundas, Ontario, Canada, and thence in later
years to the United States. His wife, Sarah
Eleanor Bayliss, was also English by birth,
her father having migrated from Stratford-
on-Avon to Rochester, New York, where he
had established himself as a merchant. The
third member of the family was Ruth, a little

girl of two years. The party met with the usual hardships and vicissitudes—the straitened life of the "covered wagon," exhaustion of men and beasts, disease, scanty supplies of food and water, exposure to storm and drought, the uncertainties of the trail, the menace of Indians, and above all the wearing monotony of the pace of walking oxen. They arrived in Weaverville, California, approximately six months from the date of their departure; and at the opening of the following year, on January 1, 1850, they reached Sacramento, which during the very period of their journey had grown from a hamlet to a thriving city of over 10,000 inhabitants. On January 16 they arrived in San Francisco just in time to witness the celebration of California's admission to statehood. This was the family into which some six years later was born the philosopher, Josiah Royce, named for his father.

In 1855 the young William James, now thirteen years of age, was again in Europe, where he remained, except for a year's interruption, until the autumn of 1860. During these five years, spent in London, Paris, Boulogne-sur-Mer, Geneva, and Bonn, he was acquiring a cosmopolitan mind, an acquaintance with languages, literature and art, and a smattering of school studies, while disproving by a series of negative experiments his father's theories of education. In 1861 he entered the Lawrence Scientific School at Harvard and turned definitively in the direction of science. His education continued to be erratic—perpetually interrupted both by ill-health and by vacillation of purpose. Before finally entering in 1875 upon his career as a teacher at Harvard he had acquired the degree of Doctor of Medicine, spent a year in South America with Agassiz, another year of study, travel, and reading in Europe, and three years of invalidism and convalescence in Cambridge.

Meanwhile, on November 20, 1855, the younger Josiah Royce was born in Grass Valley, a mining town high up in the Sierras. His father had not found gold, and was an indifferently successful storekeeper. There being no school in Grass Valley, the young Josiah derived his early instruction from his mother, a woman notable not only for her piety but for the firmness with which she preserved and handed on to her children the tradition of learning which she had imbibed at the Albion Female Seminary in Rochester. The Royce family returned to San Francisco in 1866, and although their circumstances did not improve, the young Josiah thenceforth enjoyed the advantages of continuous instruction, first at the Lincoln Grammar School and then at the Boys' High School. After some further schooling in Oakland he entered the University of California at Berkeley in the fall of 1871. It was after his graduation in 1875 that he left California for the first time, spending a year of study in Germany and two years at Johns Hopkins. It was during one of these latter years that Royce enjoyed that first interview with James at which the younger of the two confessed his intellectual yearnings and received the assurance that "a young man might rightfully devote his life to philosophy if he chose." When he returned to Berkeley as instructor in English in the autumn of 1878, he felt his isolation. "There is no philosophy," he wrote, "from Siskiyou to Ft. Yuma, and from the Golden Gate to the summit of the Sierras."[2] During the years that elapsed before 1882, when he joined James at Harvard and became his neighbor and colleague, it was to James that he continued to pour out his soul in long and frequent letters, and it was from James that he continued to receive the needed confirmation of his philosophical vocation.

2. *Idem,* I, 779, 781.

In short, while James was a product of Europe and the Atlantic seaboard, and enjoyed the advantages of ripe civilization and hereditary affluence, Royce was reared amidst the hardships and cultural poverty of the western frontier. The inborn natures of the men themselves accentuated this contrast. James was by temperament and genius peculiarly adapted to social intercourse. He was instantly and universally liked by his acquaintances, and felt himself at ease in every social situation. The amenities of life coincided with his instincts as much as with his habits, and every human contact tended to ripen into intimacy and friendship. Even in his childhood he was one of those fortunate individuals who in the midst of their fellows are happy, confident, admired, and emulated. To Royce, on the other hand, casual social relations were difficult and even painful. He was disqualified even for the normal life of a pioneer community. A youngest child and only boy, he was protected by a solicitous mother and two older sisters from the natural hazards of childhood. He must not climb a tree lest he fall, or play with the cat lest he be scratched. He was lacking in physical hardihood and had no aptitude for sports. From his earliest days he lived in an unnaturally intellectual and imaginative world of his own. When in his school days he was obliged to associate with other boys his oddity made him a target for their jibes rather than an equal associate. It is characteristic of Royce that he should have left on record this self-portrait of his early days:

About June 1866, I began to attend a large Grammar School in San Francisco. I was one of about a thousand boys. The ways of training were new to me. My comrades very generally found me disagreeably striking in my appearance, by reason of the fact that I was red-headed, freckled, countrified, quaint, and unable to play boys' games. The boys in question gave me my first introduction to the "majesty of the community." The introduction was impressively disciplinary and persistent. On the whole it seemed to me "not joyous but grievous."[3]

When Royce at the age of fifteen or thereabouts was attending the Boys' High School, he formed the acquaintance of a harmless lunatic named Norton who enjoyed delusions of grandeur and whose large red nose and apoplectic face were familiar to the residents of San Francisco. This self-appointed monarch

3. "Words of Professor Royce at the Walton Hotel at Philadelphia, December 29, 1915," *The Philosophical Review*, XXV (1916), 509.

claimed California and Mexico as his domain, and since his rule was mild it was undisputed. Royce at the age of fifteen playing chess with the Emperor Norton at the Mercantile Library in San Francisco! James at the corresponding age in gloves and high black hat walking about the streets of London with his brother Henry, or in Paris visiting the Louvre and Luxembourg and trying to paint like Delacroix! These are pictures of boyhood, but they are not essentially false even to the later years when Royce was transplanted to a New England where he was never firmly rooted, while James had fitted easily into both local and cosmopolitan communities.

The difference between the social attributes of these two men is not to be found either on the level of mere external relations, or on the level of organized society. Neither of them was promiscuously gregarious, neither of them was disposed to accept or exercise authority. They both possessed the detachment and self-reliance of thinking men, and philosophized out of the abundance of their inner lives. All the more striking the contrast of their essential social experience. To Royce intercourse with his fellowmen was difficult, and rarely perfected. It was characteristic of him that he should have cited his seminary of graduate students at Harvard as the "best concrete instance of the life of a community" with which he had become acquainted.[4] With James, on the other hand, social relations were normally effortless and life-enhancing. An expert chirographer would, no doubt, have read this difference from their handwriting—Royce's being awkward and unformed, James's fluent and graceful.

When, now, we examine the philosophical expression of these characteristic experiences, we find that each man idealized his opposite. Each praised what he lacked and coveted, taking for granted that with which by nature, inheritance, and early training he was already endowed.

Royce's moral philosophy, his religion, even his metaphysics, is an apotheosis of society. He spent his early days in rude settlements which were conscious of the value of social life because as yet they possessed none, in any but the most rudimentary sense. "My earliest recollections," he said, "included a very frequent wonder as to what my elders meant when they said that this was a new community."[5] Deeper than this vague awareness of California's social immaturity was Royce's feeling of his own personal need. From his in-

4. *Idem*, p. 511.   5. *Idem*, p. 507.

adequacy and even from the torment to which
he was subjected by his unfeeling boyhood associates, there sprang the major motive of his
philosophy. To quote his own words:

Many years later, in a lecture contained in the
first volume of my *Problem of Christianity*, I
summarized what I remember of the lesson of
the training which my schoolmates very frequently gave me, in what I there have to say
about the meaning which lies behind the Pauline
doctrine of original sin, as set forth in the sev-
enth chapter of the Epistle to the Romans. . . .
I strongly feel that my deepest motives and
problems have centered about the Idea of the
Community, although this idea has only come
gradually to my clear consciousness. This was
what I was intensely feeling, in the days when
my sisters and I looked across the Sacramento
Valley, and wondered about the great world beyond our mountains. This was what I failed to
understand when my mates taught me those instructive lessons in San Francisco. This was
that which I tried to understand when I went to
Germany. I have been unpractical,—always
socially ineffective as regards genuine "team
play," ignorant of politics, an ineffective member of committees, and a poor helper of concrete
social enterprises. Meanwhile I have always
been, as in my childhood, a good deal of a non-
conformist, and disposed to a certain rebellion.

. . . So much of the spirit that opposes the community I have and have always had in me, simply, elementally, deeply. Over against this natural ineffectiveness in serving the community, and over against this rebellion, there has always stood the interest which has taught me what I nowadays try to express by teaching that we are saved through the community.[6]

The text to which Royce here refers is the chapter entitled "The Moral Burden of the Individual," in which the Pauline doctrine of original sin is interpreted to mean that the individual man cannot save himself, but can be redeemed only by the painful impacts of a society which first hurts him and then exalts him through becoming the object of his sacrificial love. He writes:

If our social life, owing to the number, the variety, and the ignorance of the individuals who make up our social world, is prevailingly or primarily one in which strained social situations . . . are present . . . it follows that every individual who is to reach a high grade of self-consciousness as to his own doings, will be awakened to his observation of himself by one or another form or instance of social tension.[7]

James's individualistic creed found a nota-

6. *Idem*, pp. 509, 510, 511.
7. *The Problem of Christianity* (1913), I, 138.

12   William James

ble and characteristic expression in his address on "The True Harvard." Being himself
manifestly eligible for any club, he said that
"to be a college man in the mere clubhouse
sense . . . affords no guarantee of real superiority in spiritual tone." He spoke for the
"outside men":

They come from the remotest outskirts of our
country, without introductions, without school
affiliations; special students, scientific students,
graduate students, poor students of the College,
who make their living as they go. They seldom
or never darken the doors of the Pudding or the
Porcellian; they hover in the background on
days when the crimson color is most in evidence,
but they nevertheless are intoxicated and exultant with the nourishment they find here. . . .
When they come to Harvard, it is not primarily
because she is a club. It is because they have
heard of her persistently atomistic constitution,
of her tolerance of exceptionality and eccentricity, of her devotion to the principles of
individual vocation and choice. . . . The university most worthy of rational admiration is
that one in which your lonely thinker can feel
himself least lonely, most positively furthered,
and most richly fed.[8]

8. "The True Harvard," *Memories and Studies* (1911),
pp. 350, 352–353, 354.

While Royce wrote volumes to show that the lonely man needs society, James wrote articles to stress the fact that society needs loneliness. For Royce society ennobled the fragmentary individual, while for James the social waste was redeemed by its individual oases, in their rich and varied flowering. Royce idealized a community of love, in which tragic conflicts are triumphantly resolved. James idealized the irreducible differences, the obscure heroisms, the oddities of creative originality. When James intervened in human affairs it was to protest against an imperialism which crushed aspiring nationalities, or an officialdom which overruled the layman, or a formalism which killed the native spontaneities; whereas Royce's conscience was most profoundly stirred by what he construed as Germany's offense against the conscience and solidarity of mankind. Royce spoke of the "fecundity of aggregation,"[9] while James stressed the power of the erratic genius and of the thoughts which germinate in solitude. While James eulogized a primitive inwardness of life which he grasped by an act of imaginative intuition, and disparaged the urbanity which he possessed by inheritance

9. "The Mechanical, the Historical and the Statistical," *Science*, N.S., XXXIX (1914), 565.

and breeding, Royce, the rustic, dreamed of a
City of God.

There is a similar divergence and cross-cor-
respondence in the domain of religion. Both
Royce and James were profoundly influenced
by their religious inheritances. Both rejected
the specific content of that inheritance and
transformed it into a generalized attitude of
sympathy and earnestness. Both were religious in feeling, although neither was attached to any orthodoxy or institution. But
while Royce's religious inheritance came from
his mother, James's came from his father; and
while Royce's inherited religion was a literal
evangelical piety, James's was a deeply original philosophical mysticism. This divergence
had an interesting sequel. The religious philosophy of each resembled the parental prototype of the other.

Royce's mother was sustained during the
perilous crossing of the continent by prayer
and by a faith in providence. The family was
unable to attach itself to any larger group
and made their way alone, because their religious scruples forbade their travelling on the
Sabbath. In moments of gravest danger Sarah
Royce felt a sense of God's presence—"that

calm strength, that certainty of One near and all sufficient." When her family was met by a rescuing party at the foot of the Sierras, she "stood in mute adoration, breathing, in my inmost heart, thanksgiving to that Providential Hand which had taken hold of the conflicting movements, the provoking blunders, the contradictory plans, of our lives and those of a dozen other people, who a few days before were utterly unknown to each other, and many miles apart, and had from those rough, broken materials wrought out for us so unlooked for a deliverance."[10] The young Josiah was taught from the Bible, which with a copy of Milton and a small writing desk his devoted mother had brought with her from the old to the new home. He attended church with his parents until the time of his entering college. In after life his thought retained a flavor of biblical allusion and of homiletic eloquence. He took an interest in the problems of Christian theology and liked to translate his thought into the terms of Christian dogma. And yet, despite all this, the substance of his religion was philosophical rather than evangelical. God was defined as "an Absolute Ex-

10. Sarah Eleanor Royce, *A Frontier Lady*, ed. R. H. Gabriel (1932), pp. 45, 64.

perience transparently fulfilling a system of organised ideas."[11] For Royce an idea was a purpose, and in the "Absolute Experience," everything in nature and history both has a purpose and finds that purpose concretely realized. There is no stark evil, but what appears on a finite view to be stark evil is seen as a phase of moral good. Each human soul embodies a unique purpose which is an indispensable part of the meaning of the whole. Death, which seems to be a sheer defeat of that purpose, is, in the final experience, found to be a victory in disguise.

James's father, on the other hand, was religious out of the depths of his own reflection and personal experience. Like all philosophical mystics he reached God by surmounting his own thought. He did, it is true, ascribe his personal salvation to Swedenborg; but he dissociated himself utterly from the Swedenborgian sect, and nourished his mind on metaphysics. His theology was a subtle rationalization of man's alienation and return to God through the perfecting of society. God's empire was never questioned. Suffering and sin were redeemed in the eternal triumph of which they formed subordinate and essential notes. Thus

11. *The Conception of God* (1897), p. 48.

the elder James's personal religion was akin
of the philosophy of Royce.

To his son, however, he transmitted not this
"monistic" synthesis, this intellectualized certainty of cosmic goodness; but only a deep
respect for the religious experience, as worthy
of a hearing and as being a datum for which
philosophy must supply a fitting hypothesis.
And when it came to the hypothesis William
found a very different way from his father's.
Turning from the great theistic tradition of
European philosophy, from Platonism, Tho-
mism, Cartesianism, and Hegelianism, he
found his hypothesis in morbid psychology
and in that *parvenu* science known as psychi-
cal research. He took immortality to mean
quite simply and literally a prolongation of
individual life after the death of the body,
and found arguments for it in the "transmission theory," according to which the brain
does not produce the mind but lets it through
from a beyond to which, after the brain's dissolution, it may again return. In Myers's doctrine of the subliminal consciousness he saw
the possibility "that the conscious person is
continuous with a wider self through which
saving experiences come." He was not interested in any moralistic or other refined sub-

stitute for cruder religious phenomena. If he prophesied at all it was because he felt the "old Lutheran sentiment" in his bones.[12] He identified religion with the specific religious "experiences," with the spiritual adventures of saints and martyrs—with the sense of conversion, exaltation and regeneration, and with the hope of resurrection. He looked for religion among the religious in their most unmistakably religious moments, and not among the philosopher's reflections *about* religion. He justified sheer faith. He defended a " 'piecemeal' supernaturalism,"[13] or thought it the only defense of religion worth undertaking. Hence he could say to his latitudinarian friends who were much better churchgoers than himself that *he* was the methodist or evangelical, whereas they were the rationalists. It was thus James rather than Royce who could justify a literal acceptance of the piety of Royce's mother.

These characteristic religious differences between James and Royce find expression in their manner of dealing with the problem of evil. Royce had his common ground with Cal-

12. Cf. James, *Human Immortality* (1898), pp. 15 ff., 50–52; *The Varieties of Religious Experience* (1902), p. 515; Perry, *op. cit.*, II, 330.

13. James, *The Varieties of Religious Experience* (1902), p. 520.

vinism, and with the elder James, who was an
anti-Calvinistic Calvinist—a Calvinist of love
rather than of justice. It would be unjust to
Royce to say that he ignored or belittled the
fact of evil. He drank deeply from the bitter
waters of tragic experience, and felt a passionate detestation of wickedness. Nothing
could be more false to Royce than to suppose
that his Absolute was a frozen perfection. In
fact no static completeness could be true to
Royce's genius, and James is not without
fault in associating him with the notion of a
"block universe." The analogue of Royce's
Absolute is not to be found in the architectural or visual arts, but in music and literature. IIis ultimate unity of things, so far as
this was attested by his own experience, was a
moral and emotional unity.

But a unity it was, none the less. There was
a final dramatic fitness, a happy resolution.
Evil was there, bitter and painful; but it
served a purpose like the moment of discord
or the antithetical phase of dialectic. Without discord, no glorious resolution; without
temptation, no resistance; without sin, no re-
pentance; without wickedness, no triumph of
righteousness. It is reported of Royce that
once when several misfortunes befell him si-
multaneously and a friend condoled with him,

he said: "No. Each is bad, but there is a gain in having them together. They lean up against each other."[14] So in Royce's world the good and the evil leaned up against one another, and their antagonistic forces formed the arch of the moral universe.

The God of Calvin was to be loved even in his foreknowledge of the evil that will befall his creation, and the vengeance which his justice will compel him to execute. Santayana has said that

Calvinism, taken in this sense, is an expression of the agonised conscience. It is a view of the world which an agonised conscience readily embraces, if it takes itself seriously, as, being agonised, of course it must. Calvinism, essentially, asserts three things: that sin exists, that sin is punished, and that it is beautiful that sin should exist to be punished.[15]

The Absolute of Royce was not, like Calvin's God, modeled on antique ideas of criminal justice, but was, in its own characteristic terms, in terms of the tensions, conflicts, struggles, and triumphs of the moral will, an

14. George Herbert Palmer, "Josiah Royce," *Harvard Graduates' Magazine,* XXV (1916), 169.

15. *Winds of Doctrine* (1913), p. 189. Cf. Royce, *Religious Aspect of Philosophy* (1885), pp. 189–190 and *passim.*

expression of "the agonised conscience." It represented the utmost possible concession to moral dualism consistent with an ultimate philosophical monism. For in his spontaneities Royce was a moral dualist. When he identified wickedness as such he denounced it simply, without any extenuating reflection that it provided the act of denunciation with its necessary object. When, after the sinking of the *Lusitania*,[16] Royce spoke out his opinion of the Emperor William II, he felt and presented that unhappy monarch as unmixed evil and not as a counterpoise of the moral will. Nevertheless in his philosophical ethics of "loyalty" Royce invested the service of *any* cause with a moral quality, provided only that it called upon the individual for steadfastness and self-sacrifice. This appears in the words which President Roosevelt quoted on January 3, 1936, in his opening message to the second session of the Seventy-fourth Congress: "Fear not, view all the tasks of life as sacred, have faith in the triumph of the

16. Cf. Royce, "The Destruction of the *Lusitania*," *The Hope of the Great Community* (1916), esp. pp. 22–23. The text of the essay consists of extracts from one of Royce's letters to Professor L. P. Jacks, which were published in the *Hibbert Journal*, October, 1915, and, with the exception of two passages, in the London *Morning Post*, July 5, 1915.

ideal, give daily all that you have to give, be loyal, and rejoice whenever you find yourselves part of a great ideal enterprise."[17]

These words can only mean that the essence of morality lies not in the *nature* of the ideal, but in the devotion with which it is pursued. Even the ideal of virtue in the accepted sense of justice and benevolence can possess no moral merit other than that of a call to arms, an occasion to display a militant and ennobling zeal. It is not the victor that is good, but the victory: "not the absence of vice, but vice there, and virtue holding her by the throat."[18]

These last were James's words, and they are an apt statement of Royce's way of reconciling the hostility to evil with an ultimate universal harmony. As Royce had his lapses, so did James, as when he said "the solid meaning of life is always the same eternal thing,— the marriage, namely, of some unhabitual ideal, however special, with some fidelity, courage, and endurance; with some man's or woman's pains.—And, whatever or wherever life may be, there will always be the chance for that marriage to take place."[19] This idea

17. Royce, "A Word for the Times," *Harvard Graduates'. Magazine*, XXIII (1914), 208.

18. James, *The Will to Believe and Other Essays in Popular Philosophy* (1898), p. 169.

19. *Talks to Teachers on Psychology: and to Students on Some of Life's Ideals* (1899), p. 299.

that it is the loyalty that counts rather than the cause, was a monistic and Roycean conception. It is a more Jamesian James who says of evil not that it may serve the purpose of exciting "fidelity, courage, and endurance," but that it is to be utterly rejected, and hated with one's last breath: "The way of escape from evil on this system is *not* by getting it 'aufgehoben,' or preserved in the whole as an element essential but 'overcome.' *It is by dropping it out altogether, throwing it overboard and getting beyond it, helping to make a universe that shall forget its very place and name.*"[20]

Thus did Royce and James exchange parental inheritances. Royce's religious thought was akin to that of James's father; and that of James was a philosophical translation of the practical and emotional piety of Royce's mother. A similar inverse opposition of philosophy and inheritance appears in the relation of these two philosophers to their American nationality. Royce, the more American in his experience, is the more European in his philosophy; while James, the more European in his experience, is the more American in his philosophy.

20. *Pragmatism* (1907), p. 297.

Santayana once remarked that "America is a young country with an old mentality: it has enjoyed," he said, "the advantages of a child carefully brought up and thoroughly indoctrinated; it has been a wise child. But a wise child, an old head on young shoulders, always has a comic and unpromising side."[21] Although Santayana did not at the moment have him in mind, Royce illustrates the point, both outwardly and inwardly. His head was disproportionate to his shoulders, and he was in his day the most notable exponent of what Santayana called "the genteel tradition." There has always been in America an old-world philosophy to which Americans of the new world have looked for edification and for a fundamental justification of their way of life. It was once Calvinism, then deism, then the Scottish philosophy of common sense, and finally, in Royce's day, the German transcendentalism of Kant and his metaphysical successors. Royce, like James, made the acquaintance of Goethe at an early age, but where James found a serene and objective naturalism that was easily assimilable to the American mind, Royce found the Germanic "building anew of the lost universe in the

21. "The Genteel Tradition in American Philosophy," *Winds of Doctrine* (1913), p. 187.

bosom of the human spirit."[22] During his student days in Germany Royce studied Kant and Schopenhauer, and while at Johns Hopkins he gave much of his time to German literature of the Romantic period. He wrote a critical essay on Schiller as early as 1878. Among philosophers Fichte, Schelling, and Schopenhauer, and to a lesser extent Hegel, became his masters, eclipsing the Mill and Spencer of his earlier years and the Anglo-American tradition to which James gave his permanent, though qualified, allegiance.

It thus transpired that, although Royce's was the characteristic American experience, it was left to James to develop an indigenous American philosophy, the first, perhaps, in which the American experience escaped the stamp of an imported ideology. Royce, bred and reared amidst what was most unique and local in American life, imported his philosophy from the fashion makers of continental Europe; while James, uprooted almost from infancy and thoroughly imbued with the culture of Germany and France, was a philosophical patriot, cutting the garment of his thought from homespun materials and creating a new American model. Royce, the product of a raw pioneer community, conceived his universe as

22. Royce, *Spirit of Modern Philosophy* (1892), p. 100.

a perfected Absolute; James, nourished on the refinements and stabilities of advanced civilization, depicted a cosmic wilderness "game-flavored as a hawk's wing."

All "classic," clean, cut and dried, "noble," fixed, "eternal," *Weltanschauungen* seem to me to violate the character with which life concretely comes and the expression which it bears of being, or at least of involving, a muddle and a struggle, with an "ever not quite" to all our formulas, and novelty and possibility forever leaking in.[23]

Royce spent his early years in a region where people used their senses, learned by experience, and labored with their hands; his philosophy was rationalistic and *a priori*. James, born and bred among ideas, was the arch-empiricist, turning in his philosophy toward experience and practice. It was James's and not Royce's philosophical world that was "in the making"; it was James's and not Royce's conclusion, that "there is no conclusion." Royce took refuge in "the Eternal"; while for James time, flux, and chance constituted the very pulse of the living reality. Royce, feeling his physical impotence in a world of struggle, asked to have the victory

23. Perry, *op. cit.*, II, 700.

written in the stars in order to contemplate
and relive it in imagination. James, on the
other hand, was the realist. To apply James's
own expressions, it was Royce who in philosophy was "the tender-foot Bostonian," though
he originated even west of the Rocky Mountains; while James himself, who frequented
Boston, Newport, and the capitals of Europe,
was the philosophical "Rocky Mountain
tough." James's "tough-mindedness," like
the "tender-mindedness" of Royce, dwelt in
the realm of philosophic thought, but his
thinking took the form of an imaginative contrast to the comparative security of his actual
condition. That which gave him "a sort of
deep enthusiastic bliss" was a sense of "active
tension," a sense, as he expressed it, "of holding my own . . . and trusting outward things
to perform their part . . . but without any
guaranty that they will."[24]

That the American element in Royce's
philosophy—his empiricism and his practi-
calism—is always in the last analysis subor-
dinated to the requirements of his imported
idealism, while James's nostalgic American-
ism is dominant and incorrigible, appears in
their philosophies of evil. James's dualism

24. *The Letters of William James* (1920), I, 199–200.

and meliorism is the view which might be expected of a man whose philosophy reflected
the American conquest of nature and confi-
dence in the future, Royce's optimistic monism is the speculative solution of a man
steeped in the European tradition.

The same contrast appears in their belated,
though none the less profound disagreement
over pragmatism. In the early days when they
held their philosophical conversation by letters exchanged between Cambridge and California, and in the first years of their association at Harvard, James and Royce were both
interested in what the former referred to as
"the motives of philosophizing." While to
James, at least, the question first presented
itself as psychological, it ultimately had a
profound philosophical import for them both.
It was at one and the same time their strongest philosophical bond and the occasion of
their greatest divergence. To raise the question of the motives which actuate thinking
implies that *thought is actuated by motives,*
and is not, as intellectualists are accustomed
to suppose, a mere passive effect of perception or a forced acceptance of inexorable necessity. We think for practical reasons, that
is, because of something that we hope by

thought to attain. From this view it is a short
step to a theory of truth: to the theory,
namely, that truth is an adverb of the pur-
posive activity of thought, or an adjective of
the ideas which this activity employs, and not
an honorific substantive used to designate the
reality thought about. Thought is true in
proportion as its purpose is realized, and
ideas are true in proportion as they serve the
purpose for which thought employs them. It
is a further corollary of this view that thought
chooses *what* reality shall become its object.
In short, thought is true when it thinks successfully about that which it chooses to think
about; or, a thought is to be judged true or
false relatively to its own specific and inherent claims.

On this seemingly identical ground both
philosophers took their stand. But it soon
transpired that they meant something very
different. In short, their common profession
of voluntarism served only to make more
manifest the difference between the intellectualism of the one and the empiricism of the
other.

It may appear paradoxical to describe a
voluntarist as an intellectualist, since voluntarism means the priority of will over intellect. But no student of the history of philoso-

phy will be shocked. Being familiar with his
Kant and his Fichte, he knows that it is possible so to intellectualize the will in advance
that its victory over intellect is only a victory
of intellect in one guise over intellect in another. The intellectual part of man is subor-
dinated not to sheer will, to pure appetite,
passion, or impulsion, but to a preferred
will, a privileged will, a will already legitimated. And the test of its legitimacy is its rationality. It is a will pledged to universality,
to consistency, to completeness, to truth. This
being the case it is intellect and not will that
has the last word. In other words, to subordinate the theoretical reason to the practical
reason is to subordinate both theory and practice to reason.

In Royce the legitimate will is not only an
intellectualized, idealized will, but it is a metaphysical will, a will whose realization is a *fait
accompli:* so that all private and natural wills
find their ought-to-be in what everlastingly
is. The ultimate constitution of the universe
conforms to the requirements of my intellect,
and if I attempt to deny this I can only deny
it in the name of the intellect and thus rein-
state the same requirements. Thus while
"everything finite and temporal is," as Royce
says, "practical," the sting of this bold af-

firmation is at once drawn by the further affirmation, "all that is practical borrows its truth from the Eternal."[25]

Royce's complaint against James is, in effect, that he has failed so to define practice as to confine it to theoretical ends. He complains, in short, that James *really* reduced theory to practice, instead of reducing it to a form of practice into which the demands of theory have already been incorporated. Theory is to obey the requirements of practice, provided practice has already agreed to require only what is agreeable to theory.

This appears very clearly in Royce's assessment of James's pragmatism in his *Philosophy of Loyalty*. He affirms his general agreement that truth is "practical," but insists upon applying an intellectual norm to the practical. The truth is what satisfies my will when I will consistently, and when I will the "whole":

I fully agree . . . that whenever a man asserts a truth, his assertion is a deed,—a practical attitude, an acknowledgment of some fact. . . . I myself, as a teacher of philosophy, have for years insisted upon viewing truth in this practical way. . . . I was taught this by . . . Kant,

25. "The Eternal and the Practical," *Philosophical Review*, XIII (1904), 142.

Fichte, Hegel, and Professor James himself.
. . . For Professor James's pragmatism, despite its entertaining expressions of horror of the eternal, actually does state one aspect of eternal truth. It is, namely, eternally true that all search for truth is a practical activity, with an ethical purpose. . . . The attainment of truth means success. . . . But the genuine success that we demand is an ethical success. . . . We need unity of life. In recognizing that need my own pragmatism consists. . . . Our loyalty to truth is a hint of this unity. . . . The real whole conspectus of experience, the real view of the totality of life, the real expression of that will to live in and for the whole, which every assertion of truth and every loyal deed expresses —well, it must be a conspectus that includes whatever facts are indeed facts, be they past, present, or future. I call this whole of experience an eternal truth. I do not thereby mean, as my colleague seems to imagine, that the eternal first exists, and that then our life in time comes and copies that eternal order. I mean simply that the whole of experience includes all temporal happenings, contains within itself all changes, and, since it is the one whole that we all want and need, succeeds in so far as it supplements all failures, accepts all, even the blindest of services, and wins what we seek. Thus winning it is practically good and worthy. But if one insists, How do you know all this? I reply:

I know simply that to try to deny the reality of this whole of truth is simply to reaffirm it.[26]

For James, all wills stand in the last analysis on the same footing, all passions and demands possess indefeasible claims. Any idea that satisfies a passion or demand possesses on that account some measure of truth. There is then a multiplicity and rivalry of historic truths, legitimated by the actual uses which they serve. There is no "eternal truth" to displace them, because there is no one preferred will which displaces all others. Even the acknowledgment of facts, or the love of wholeness, unity and consistency have to take their place along with the rest. These and like passions may, if one wishes, be set apart and called theoretic; but when one comes to ask why these passions, so denominated, should take precedence over others, then it is a question of matching passion against passion. The problem is transferred from theoretic to practical grounds, and becomes the problem of solving a conflict of interest, and of finding some sort of comprehensive or maximum satisfaction.

Royce felt that pragmatism raised a *moral* issue. It substituted expediency for principle,

26. Royce, *The Philosophy of Loyalty* (1908), pp. 324–327, 340, 341, 342, 344–345.

and Royce took the liberty of confusing truth with veracity in order to express his moral disapproval more effectively. He imagined a pragmatist on the witness stand, taking his oath as follows: "I promise to tell whatever is expedient and nothing but what is expedient, so help me future experience."[27] According to Royce the judgment of truth possessed the solemnity of a moral judgment. "This is true," means "This satisfies my conscience," or "This I feel morally obliged to say." Hence the tragic note in Royce's later relations to James, his painful sense that James was not merely mistaken, but delinquent, or at least reprehensibly frivolous.[28] It is easy to understand why Royce should have been shocked and pained at what he thought to be the opportunism and light-mindedness of James's pragmatism. But it is likewise easy to understand why James should have felt that Royce at some point introduced a dogmatic preference, or surrendered to the spell of edification.

The major philosophical difference between James and Royce is a difference of ethics. For both men even the truth of science is relative to the will of the thinker. To find the fundamental difference, then, we must look in that

27. *Idem*, p. 331.
28. Cf. Perry, *op. cit.*, I, 820–821.

quarter. For Royce, the *a priorist* and abso-
lutist, there is a will which transcends the
natural inclinations, and which imposes upon
them the principle of loyalty to the "whole."
This is his *a priorism*. The moral ideal is
metaphysically enshrined: the world *is* eternally what its temporal and finite parts aspire
to be. This is Royce's absolutism. James, on
the other hand, is a utilitarian—in the broad
sense of that term. Moral value is rooted in
the natural desires of men. The good rests on
the experience of interests and of the means
or objects by which they find themselves satisfied. The maximum of satisfaction, the
"richer universe," the "more inclusive order,"
"the *best whole*, in the sense of awakening the
least sum of dissatisfactions," is a regulative
principle of conduct, and its realization is a
future possibility contingent on the success
of the moral will.[29] The real world contains
this aspiration and struggle, and does not exclude its attainment in time. But for James
even the highest moral truths are empirical
and experimental.

THE fascination of biography lies in the elusive mystery of personality. There is an ultimate flavor, a spiritual physiognomy, that

29. James, *The Will to Believe* (1898), p. 205.

remains after the analysis has been made, and
after every tributary influence has been traced
and named. Royce was a lonely and imper-
fectly adapted man, singing the praises of a
perfect society; a product of the American
frontier, philosophizing after the manner of
Germany. The son of a simply pious mother,
he developed an elaborately metaphysical religion; reared in a new society which placed a
premium upon hazardous enterprise, he took
refuge in the Eternal; born in a practical
world, he repudiated utility and moralized in
terms of absolute duty. James, who was per-
fectly socialized by inheritance, breeding, and
inborn aptitude, who was cosmopolitan in experience, who was the son of a philosophic
mystic, who enjoyed economic security, possessed the taste of an artist and enjoyed every
opportunity of leisurely cultivation—this
James, so conditioned by experience, became
in his philosophy individualistic, patriotic,
evangelical, adventurous, and pragmatic.

When all this has been said, and imputed
to that strange force which leads men in their
philosophy to surmount and compensate their
personal experience, there remains the fact
that Royce was Royce and James was James
in some residual sense. This last nucleus of

personality I can only seek to present as I remember it myself.

Royce was ponderous and James was agile.
The effect of thinking in the case of Royce
was to complicate the simple, whereas James
simplified the complex. Santayana has written that Royce was an "overworked, standard-
ised, academic engine, creaking and thump-
ing on at the call of duty or of habit, with no
thought of sparing itself or any one else."[30] I
have not that impression, or at any rate I
should not so express it. I should say rather
that Royce had a high viscosity of thought; a
cumbersomeness of discourse that achieved
distinction by a kind of laborious eloquence.
His thought must always be cosmic, and attempt to envisage wholes too large for any
finite mind. If he said too much, it was because
his ideas were so vastly extended that no fin-
ished paragraph could ever contain them. His
very learning was a cargo, which he carried
with him always. Hence John Jay Chapman
has suggested that "if only he had never been
taught to read, Royce would have been a very
great man."[31] In short, Royce was in a meas-

30. *Character and Opinion in the United States* (1920),
p. 98.
31. "Portrait of Josiah Royce," *The Outlook*, CXXII
(1919), 372.

ure immobilized by the accumulation of his intellectual possessions. That the first effect was overpowering is the testimony of all his pupils and friends. Chapman has recorded this sense of Royce's weight and inexhaustible resourcefulness:

He was spherical, armed cap-a-pie, sleepless, and ready for all comers. . . . Royce was the John L. Sullivan of philosophy. . . . He was very extraordinary and knew everything and was a bumble-bee—a benevolent monster of pure intelligence, zigzagging, ranging, and uncatchable. I always had this feeling about Royce— that he was a celestial insect. . . . Time was nothing to him. He was just as fresh at the end of a two-hours' disquisition as at the start. Thinking refreshed him. The truth was that Royce had a phenomenal memory; his mind was a card-indexed cyclopaedia of all philosophy. . . . His extreme accessibility made him a sort of automat restaurant for Cambridge. He had fixed hours when any one could resort to him and draw inspiration from him.[32]

Chapman has also described a certain occasion when Royce was invited to his son's room at Harvard:

Royce would not remove his coat or sit down; and he talked for an hour. He began with the

32. *Idem*, pp. 372, 377.

Norse legends, to illustrate the German spirit. He recited with wonderful skill a poem of Edgar Allan Poe's, and he must, first and last, have mentioned about everything that could be thought of between Odin and Poe. The rest of us sat rapt and happy. There was a weight and atmospheric pressure in the room. In our minds floated memories of the great talkers of history. Perhaps Coleridge may have talked like this, or Bacon.[33]

With James there was no such impression either of volume or of endurance. Measured by these standards he felt most acutely his own inferiority to Royce. He read much, but he had forgotten most of it—transformed it into a quality of mind, or a residuum of apt allusion. His lectures were halting and intermittently forceful. He was spontaneously brilliant, redeeming periods of awkward hesitancy with momentary flashes of insight, disturbingly fresh observations, and infallibly apt descriptions. He struggled for truth with infinite patience, but communicated the results and not the process. He was a conversationalist rather than a talker, adapting his ideas and their expression with instantaneous flexibility to the responsive sympathy of unlearned minds. He thought of one thing at a

33. *Idem*, p. 377.

time, and let the whole take care of itself; believing like a true pluralist and empiricist
that if the universe was to be subjugated it
would not be by a single speculative stroke,
but by adding truth to truth until its length
and breadth and depth were compassed.

With this difference between the whole-to-
part, totalitarian thinking of Royce, and
James's method of part-to-whole particular-
ism, was associated the fact that Royce's acts
and feelings were so completely infused with
his thought that he seemed always to be wearing the toga of the philosopher. James, on the
other hand, usually appeared in citizens'
clothes. He was secular minded, and spoke as
one layman to another. Both men were fond of
nonsense, but James's nonsense was pure nonsense, whereas Royce's, like that of Lewis
Carroll, whom he so liked to quote, had a
deeper meaning. Even in his domestic affections there was wont to be some trace of philosophic wisdom and detachment, as when he
made the following entry in his diary:

The afternoon over Helmholtz's *Physiological
Optics,* with references to the *Hermann's Physiology* on the same subject. All this carried on
while sitting on the floor with C., K. being absent on a calling expedition. Baby is compan-
ionable, but does not interfere with my work,

wanting merely somebody near by and on equal terms.[34]

The essential difference between the mind of Royce and the mind of James was reflected in their attitudes to nature and art. Royce was deeply and permanently impressed by the grand scale of the California landscape which he loved to contemplate. When he sought contact with nature he went to sea. Now when one goes to sea one is carried in a ship, and as a passenger enjoys the vast expanse of sky and water. In art it was music, and especially symphonic music with its complexity, volume, and emotional depth, which made to him the strongest appeal. His style was massive and sluggish. When James, on the other hand, enjoyed nature, he climbed mountains on his own feet, or sought to recapture the primitive intimacies of animal life. In the arts it was the finite and discriminated plastic form which most exalted him. In his style he was terse, nervous, dynamic, lucid, and forceful. He said the particular thing that was on his mind, or was revealed in his experience, and said it tellingly.

The idiosyncrasies that divided Royce and James enhanced their friendship. They en-

34. Tuesday, January 16, 1883.

joyed and enriched one another's differences.
Kindness and the hatred of cruelty were the
deepest moral passion in both men. Their
friendship was further based on neighborly
intimacy, and above all on a common quality
of high-mindedness. James was thirteen years
older than Royce, and his attitude was colored
by chivalry, as was Royce's by gratitude and
respect. But at bottom they were bound by
the fact that each recognized the other's
zestful and generous tolerance. When they
walked back to their neighboring homes on
Irving Street, or standing at the gate prolonged their talk into the darkening hours,
there was indeed a "fecundity of aggregation." But the aggregation was a meeting of
two independent and irreducible individuals,
sensitized to one another by reciprocal love
and esteem.

It is an occasion both of marvel and of re-
joicing that love requires no twinship and little duplication. For love is essentially a duality; an exchange of gifts and not a fusion
or dissolution of terms. Granting tolerance
and kindness, and a capacity for endearment
by association, there is no limit to the differences by which it may be fructified. Like the
lightning which strikes across from cloud to
cloud it bridges an interval between two shad-

owy depths. It is a new circuit of energy which springs from two regions of potentiality, creating light and heat and motion; but it enhances and never exhausts its separate sources. The happy miracle lies not in unity alone, but in the association of unity with polarity, tension, and surprise.

CHAPTER II

AN EMPIRICAL THEORY
OF KNOWLEDGE

CONSIDERED in its most general aspect
the philosophy of William James is an
empiricism, or philosophy of experience. This
is at one and the same time the mark of its
British ancestry and its chief qualification for
acceptance by the modern world. Being with
singular whole-heartedness dedicated to the
doctrine of empiricism, James's philosophy is
peculiarly qualified to exemplify its genius.

James's theory of knowledge illustrates a
duality in empiricism, which being brought
into clear view turns out to be not an ambi-
guity of carelessness, but rather a two-sided-
ness inherent in the nature of any doctrine
which takes experience as its standard. For
human experience is less than human knowledge, and there must, therefore, be two types
of knowledge: that which lies *within* experience, and that which passes *beyond*. This difference is recognized by James in his distinction between "knowledge by acquaintance" and
"knowledge about," a distinction which he in
turn borrowed from John Grote, and explic-

itly affirmed and amplified as early as 1884.[1] It is James's essential and characteristic contention that while both kinds of knowledge are indispensable, knowledge by acquaintance is completer and more conclusive than knowledge about, the latter being a substitute or adjunct which is required in order to overcome the limited range of the former. Knowledge is consummated when it coincides with reality, and that consummation occurs only in experience.

In order to understand precisely what James means by acquaintance, it is necessary to consider not only this broader difference between knowledge within experience and knowledge without, but also a second duality which is inherent in experience itself.

The significance of the notion of experience arises from its antithesis to ideas. Thus the word "tree" means the idea of a "woody perennial plant having a single main axis or stem (trunk), commonly exceeding 10 feet in height and usually devoid of branches below, but bearing a head of branches and foliage or a crown of leaves at the summit."[2] This ideal

1. William James, "The Function of Cognition," reprinted in *The Meaning of Truth* (1909), pp. 11ff.
2. *Webster's New International Dictionary of the English Language* (1910), p. 2191.

meaning carries us far, and for considerable
stretches of life no other meaning is required.
But there is another meaning of the word
"tree," analogous to what is known among
logicians as "denotation" in contrast with
"connotation." In this second sense the question of the meaning of "tree" is answered by
saying: "that is a tree." The "that" contained
in this answer,—the look of the tree, its over-
thereness, its place, direction, and presence,
its side-by-sideness, its fragrance, the feel of
it, the sound of the wind in its branches, the
direct dealing with it—in short, its occurrence
in perception, affection, and action--is the
"experience" of the tree. Empiricism of
James's type insists that there *is* such a tree-
experience. The term "that" in the above answer is not a *mere* word. It is what the demon-
strative pronoun demonstrates: specific *qualia*
of color, shape, size, position, time, odor, distance, activity, grace, and texture, all com-
posing a specific individuality which is thereafter familiar and recognizable. The tree of
experience is the tree thus apprehended in its
native terms—freshly, originally, intimately,
personally, directly, contemporaneously, or
presentatively; as distinguished from the tree
as known absently, remotely, indirectly, or
representatively. So far acquaintance is the

knowledge afforded by experience itself, as distinguished from that which is afforded by ideas.

But experience in this general sense has itself a further duality. There is, on the one hand, *that which* is presented. And there is, on the other hand, the *occurrence* of the presentation. On the one hand, experience is revealing—it shines by its own luminosity, as opposed to those secondary entities such as plans, words, symbols, and concepts which reflect its light. On the other hand, it is contingent, occurring as something dynamic and external. I may myself "represent" the tree, but I do not myself present it; it presents itself—*to* me, and prescribes the conditions of action. Thus a clap of thunder exhibits the original quality of thunderousness, while at the same time intruding itself unbidden upon the sentient mind. In other words, experience *conveys* or *discloses*, and experience is *given*, or *imposed*.

It is generally assumed that sensation is experience *par excellence*, and that empiricism is the philosophy of sensation. This assertion is true only in a highly qualified sense. It is no part of James's empiricism to reduce the concreteness of experience to sensational atoms, still less to limit the *qualia* of experience to

the "six senses." Nevertheless, sensation remains for James, as for all empiricists, the
prototype of experience, defining the plane
upon which experience lies, and exhibiting the
characteristics of experience preëminently. It
is significant, therefore, that sensation possesses an inner duality whose components di-
verge at so wide an angle that if one were to
follow each to the exclusion of the other they
would lead to opposite philosophical conclusions. Sensation signifies two things. On the
one hand, it presents that scene of color,
sound, taste, and smell which constitutes the
panorama of human life. But, on the other
hand, sensation is something that happens to a
man, and of which he must take practical account. It signifies an impact from the environment—a thrust from without; which may intrude upon the flow of thought and block the
will, or be accepted as a welcome gift, or suf-
fered tolerantly as an accompaniment and
background of existing activity, or be used or
resisted by an appropriate form of behavior.

Now when these two dualities are brought
together the full complexity of an empirical
theory of knowledge is revealed. Some knowledge is immediate, consisting in actual experience, while other knowledge is "mediate," consisting in substitutions for, or anticipations of,

immediacy. But immediate experience is two-
fold, embracing both revelations and givenness; and there will be a corresponding duality of mediate or representative knowledge.
On the one hand, there will be those intermediaries which represent revelation; and on the
other hand, those which represent givenness.
Both, according to James, are anticipations
of experience constituting an advanced readiness for it when and where it comes, and both
possess relations within themselves, which constitute the processes of thinking. In both cases
there are, therefore, two kinds of truth—the
truth which the intermediaries have relatively
to one another, through their mutual consistency or implication; and the truth which they
have relatively to the experiences which they
anticipate. Of them both it may be said that
the first or *a priori* kind of truth, the truth of
thinking, is subordinate to the latter or *a pos-
teriori* kind of truth, the truth of fact. The
verdict of experience is final, and any other
verdict is provisional.

So much may be said of all empiricism. But
the difference between the two aspects leads,
at least *prima facie*, to a divergence between
empirical schools. The anticipation of revelation is an expectation on the part of man's
theoretic faculties. He expects to sense or feel

this or that specific quality or congeries of qualities. When the revealing experience occurs, it is *what* he expected, *what* he was *looking* for, and is accompanied by a sense of familiarity. This provides the test of the truth of his anticipation. Thus the idea of the tree prepares the knower who entertains it for the upright, leaf-crowned form which springs from the earth to a height exceeding human stature. The givenness of experience, on the other hand, is anticipated in plans of action, in operations devised in advance of which the event of experience provides the complementary external condition. The occurrence of this condition makes it possible to complete the operations, and this serves as the test of truth. Thus the idea of the tree as contained in the above definition prepares the knower to sit in the shade of the tree, or to fell it and convert it into lumber, or to apply a foot-rule to it end over end with some remainder left. We have, therefore, two types of empiricism, the intuitive or contemplative, in which experience is revelation and thought is foresight; and the practical, in which experience is givenness and thought is an experiment or planned operation.

The practical type of empiricism, in which experience is givenness, and the idea is a planned operation in which the reactions of experience are anticipated, reaches its culmination in modern experimental science, and in that cult of positivism in which the procedure of science is taken as the ideal form of knowledge.

The essence of the experimental method in physical science is the acceptance of a determinate sensory event as constituting the final verification or proof to which every theory must be submitted. A sensory event is deduced from a hypothesis—an event such, for example, as the coincidence in a certain line of vision of a needle with a mark on a recording apparatus and according as this event does or does not occur, the hypothesis is deemed true or false. The verification derives its validity from the contingency, externality, or *givenness* of experience. The scientist may display a high degree of initiative and creative imagination in the formulation of the theory, but the verification must be taken as it comes, with complete renunciation and submission. The scientist may devise and manipulate his instruments, but if he interferes with the verification it loses all its force and the scientist has been unfaithful to his task.

Granting that this is a somewhat simplified version of the experimental method, the fact remains that so far as that method is concerned the important thing about a sensation is its occurrence or non-occurrence under certain conditions—the permission or coöperation which it accords to a projected operation. This implies, of course, that the occurring event shall be somehow identified. But it would serve the purpose equally well if this identification were indirect. It is not, in short, absurd to imagine a verifying machine, in which the hypothesis might be inserted, and which would then print it or return it to its author, according as the crucial sensory event did or did not occur. For the sensory event has a specific physical component or "stimulus," and this can be converted into mechanical equivalents.

When the test is positive, the result is the truth of the *theory*, and the theory is framed in terms of mathematical or experimental "operations." As such true theories become more comprehensive by extension and generalization, there results a conceptualized and mechanical universe which bears no resemblance whatever to the "world of the senses." In short, the tendency of experimentalism is to reduce sensation to a nod of "yes" or "no" —to the role of merely accepting or rejecting a construction which has been framed in advance in terms of physical and symbolic instruments.

The progress of the experimental art and its technological fruitfulness have led in modern times to claims of exclusive sovereignty over the territory of human knowledge and ignorance. Science, having come to understand its own method, and being thus authorized to say that what is not strictly mathematico-experimental shall not bear the name of "science," then proceeds to the bolder assertion that what is not "science" is not knowledge—or that a question which cannot ultimately be answered in strictly mathematico-experimental terms is not a proper question at all.

In fact, however, any question is legitimate which is answerable, and any question is answerable which prescribes a determinate satisfaction. A question is a state of doubt or curiosity, and if the doubt is capable of being resolved, or if the curiosity is capable of being appeased, even imaginatively, then that question is a legitimate question. To define legitimate questions in any narrower terms is a tyrannical denial of that right which every human claim has to its own realization.

Now the question which is characteristic of

physical science is the technological question:
the discovery of those forms of organized activity, symbolic or physical, which the external environment permits and completes. As
physical science develops, this motive is increasingly purified, and the answers which it
finds become more irrelevant to other and
equally legitimate forms of inquiry. Its terms
become more technical, that is, appropriate
to its own exclusive purpose. The occurrence
and non-occurrence of events under certain
conditions, and the degree of their occurrence,
are detected and measured by instruments of
increasing precision. Complex relationships
formulated in logic and mathematics tend to
take the place of qualitative specificities and
changes. Explanation supersedes description.
The content of scientific knowledge becomes
increasingly *a priori*, that is, prescribed in
advance of the facts by the requirements of
experimental procedure. Nature is replaced
by the laboratory. Nothing which is discovered outside of a laboratory is called science,
and it is part of the code of science that no
question shall be asked in the laboratory
which cannot be answered in the laboratory:
which means that no question shall be asked
to which sensory events, mechanically con-
trolled and therefore repeatable at will, can-

not give an answer of "yes" or "no." It might, I think, be said that positivism tends to a sort of *reductio ad absurdum* in which there is nothing left of the so-called world except interrogative sentences, together with a *Ding an sich* to which they are addressed, and which delivers gestures of acceptance or rejection.

Meanwhile, however, there are other questions which demand satisfaction. What ought I to do? What is this or that "like"? What is the character of the world when all experiences are assembled? What of the ultra-scientific grounds on which positivism itself, or any other philosophy of science, rests? When the limiting characteristics of the special sciences are noted and discounted, what is the effect of this correction? These and other questions have their appropriate answers. The philosophies of the past have satisfied the needs felt by those who have asked them. Where the needs remain unsatisfied it is possible to imagine the sort of answer which would satisfy them. To deny to such questions and answers the status of science means nothing more than that, being different questions, they cannot be answered in the same manner as those questions which one chooses to call scientific questions. There can be no objection to a limiting definition of science, but contempo-

rary positivism is not guiltless of that equivo-
cation which is characteristic of all positivisms old and new. The term "science" is used
to mean knowledge of a specific sort, governed
and restricted by its own proper motive; but
also to mean knowledge in a eulogistic sense,
so that when it is shown that a certain question is not capable of being answered "scientifically" it is forthwith disparaged. A
completely undogmatic positivism, a positivistic positivism, would restrict itself to a definition of the sort of knowledge exemplified in
physics, and a demonstration that knowledge
of this sort can be extended into the fields of
other sciences. Such a positivism would be
consistent with any judgment whatsoever as
to the *dignity* of physical knowledge. It might
appear in the sequel that science, so conceived
and limited, constituted the ideal norm by
which all knowledge should be appraised, or
that it was shallow and trivial.

Contemporary positivism, together with all
those doctrines of scientific methodology
which call themselves by such names as "instrumentalism" or "operationalism," represents the destiny of science to confine itself
more and more strictly to experimental prediction and control. With this riper development of the practical type of empiricism

James would be largely in agreement, as he was in agreement with its earlier and to him contemporary stages, represented by Mach, Poincaré, and Karl Pearson. James's pragmatism embraces his version of experimentalism. If his pragmatism differs from contemporary positivism it is because, being a philosopher by training and inheritance, he felt responsible for its implications. Contemporary positivisms are satisfied with such terms as "instrument" or "operation," and are even known to use the term "pragmatic," as though this were the end of the matter. James, like Dewey and other philosophers who have adopted the experimentalist view of science, accepted its full consequences and sought to make them explicit. He realized that a practical empiricism bases theory on practice, and introduces a norm of usefulness as the higher sanction of such immediate norms of verifiability, simplicity, consistency, or scrupulosity as suffice within the confines of the laboratory. This usefulness has itself to be justified in ethical terms, either as an ultimate ethical axiom or as a secondary principle derived from some other ethical premise. James's practical empiricism differs from positivism, then, only in being more thorough and more alive to the philosophical eventualities. He would no doubt find occasion today to repeat what in 1888 he wrote to the psychologist Ribot:

Empirical facts without "metaphysics" will always make a confusion and a muddle. I'm sorry to hear you still disparage metaphysics so much, since rightly understood, the word means only the search for *clearness* where common people do not even suspect that there is any lack of it. The ordinary positivist has simply a bad and muddled metaphysics which he refuses to criticize or discuss.[3]

But that which distinguishes James's empirical philosophy radically from positivism, or from any mere experimentalism, is his recognition of another sort of knowledge altogether. This other sort of knowledge proceeds from that essential duality of experience which has been remarked. Experience provides not only practical tests, which verify or reject hypotheses of action, but vistas of the actual world which realize or disappoint intuitive expectations. James goes further. The intuitive expectation is more *fundamental* than the experimental hypothesis. The latter is a preparation of action for the givenness of events, but this is to be construed as a prepa-

3. From an unpublished letter in the James Collection in the Widener Library, Harvard University.

ration for that intuition which when it occurs is the proper and exciting occasion for action. An automobile driver approaching an intersection of streets is prepared to stop or to accelerate his car to suit the contingency of the traffic light. But this means that he is primarily prepared for the intuitions of green and red, and only secondarily for the appropriate motor responses.

To attain perfect clearness in our thoughts of an object . . . we need only consider what . . . sensations we are to expect from it, and what reactions we must prepare. . . . The ultimate test for us of what a truth means is indeed the conduct it dictates or inspires. But it inspires that conduct because it first foretells some particular turn to our experience which shall call for just that conduct from us.[4]

In other words, the practical aspect of experience is the sequel to its intuitive aspect, since the latter "calls" for and evokes the former. Similarly, the "reactions prepared" owe their propriety to the sensations or other qualitative immediacies expected.

To this priority of the intuitive to the practical aspect in both presentation and representation is added the priority of presentation

4. James, *Collected Essays and Reviews* (1920), pp. 411, 412.

to representation,—the priority of actual experience over all its anticipations, whether intuitive or practical. "Adequate" knowledge, rarely attained, is a "conflux or identification, such as common sense assumes in sense perception where the sensation *is* the object." All other knowledge, though it *is* knowledge, and comprises the greater part of what is so designated, is "symbolic," pointing toward the object and uniquely related to it, but more or less remotely. Even the representation is more adequate when it *resembles* the presentation for which it prepares. Other persons are adequately known in proportion as sympathy or telepathy permits the knower to *identify* himself with their experiences.[5] It is the purpose of knowledge to apprehend some portion of reality. But realities *are* what they are "known as," when knowledge assumes the form of immediate experience.[6] Thus acquaintance, construed as *experience in its aspect of revelation*, constitutes knowledge in the ultimately preferred sense.

One further point. When ideas are verified, this *might* be interpreted to mean that the verifying experience merely certifies the knowledge contained in the idea. The verify-

5. Cf. Perry, *op. cit.*, II, 538–540.
6. Cf. James, *Pragmatism* (1907), p. 50.

ing experience itself contributes nothing but a confirmation of the knowledge already existing. If the experience does not occur, nothing is lost except the assurance of truth, which might conceivably be obtained in some other way, as, for example, from authority. Or one might express this by saying that verification by experience adds nothing to knowledge, except the knowledge that it is knowledge. The verification of the idea of the tree conveys no further information or understanding of the tree, but only the theoretic right to affirm the idea as it stands. When, however, as with James, the idea is only an imperfect substitute or foretaste or signboard, rendered necessary by the regrettable absence of experience, then that experience when it comes not only certifies but supersedes the idea. It is the cognitive consummation. It is not only a proof of the cognitive value of the idea, but a development of the idea into something cognitively better. It is cognitive, and superlatively cognitive, in its own right. Reality, taken as the counterpart of the culminating knowledge, is *as experience perceives* and not *as ideas conceive.*

Thus acquaintance, construed as the sensing or feeling of what any given subject matter is "like," speaks the last word in knowledge. When we say that a man who has never had the experience of being in love lacks something of knowledge, we do not mean merely that there is something he has not lived through—that there are adventures and shocks which have not happened to him, and that he lacks that expertness which comes from practice—we mean that for lack of the experience in question he does not know what love *is*, lacks familiarity with its qualitative essence, and would have a sense of complete novelty were it to swim into his ken. When he hears or reads of "love" he is familiar with the relation of that to other words, and he can draw inferences from that concept to other concepts. He may be able to deal with love when he meets it. But he is unable to pass from the word, concept, or procedure to its original. He moves on a level of logical and practical meanings and cannot pass from this to the plane of feeling, and recover that specific emotion which is love in itself. He may regret this, and may long to know what love is like, in which case he must manage somehow to be in love. Wishing to know, and finding this way of knowing, he may then say, "Ah! Now I understand."

Or take the parallel case of sensation. The color-blind person may be so well versed in the

science of color that he can produce any color
at will and elaborate the whole system of chro-
matic inferences. The physics, the physiology,
the technique, and even the psychology of
color he can master—wave lengths, spectrum,
rods and cones, color pyramid and paint—but
of the "look" of colors and their immediate
visual selves he will, for all his science, know
less than the normal child. And when I say
"know," I use the term advisedly, meaning
that he will feel an interrogative craving for
which there is an appointed satisfaction which
others than himself have found.

It is a mistake to suppose that knowledge
of this sort is inarticulate. The common objection to immediate knowledge, receiving its
classical formulation in Kant's doctrine that
all cognitive experience assumes the form of
judgment, is beside the point. If the discovery
of love should express itself in the words "So
this is love!"; or if the transition from blind-
ness to vision should be accompanied by the
comment, "I wonder what this color is that I
have heard talked about . . . Ah! this must
be it!" a distinguishable moment of acquaintance would still remain. It is not converted
into concepts merely because it is anticipated
by them—conceptually framed and conceptually described. If it comes, it comes. The lov-

ingness of love or the greenness of green possess their recognizable specificity even amidst diverse conceptual and practical contexts.

It will serve to distinguish the knowledge in which this moment of acquaintance remains unreduced, if we compare it with the case in which it *is* reduced. The color green may be described as that color, *whatever it is,* which occupies the place on the spectrum between yellow and blue. The visual immediacy is here eliminated, and replaced by *the color between yellow and blue,* or *the fourth color from the left-hand end of the spectrum.* If, on the other hand, I wish to know what green is like, and am told that it is the color between yellow and blue on the spectrum, then the conceptual description serves not to replace the immediacy, but to point it out. It constitutes a rule of procedure by which he who would know what green is can find it for himself. If, having obeyed the rule, I make the discovery, the moment of acquaintance has been reached by means of concepts, but being reached, it speaks for itself and no longer needs the guide which has pointed the way.

When knowledge of this sort is accorded its full rights and is generalized as a philosophical maxim, it comes to this: that all words and concepts have an ultimate meaning in terms

of some character which is discerned by acquaintance, and which is inaccessible to minds
not attuned by some sensitive or affective faculty rightly directed by an act of attention.
Behavior, both verbal discourse and overt
action, can dispense with these ultimates, con-
fining itself to their symbolic substitutes, and
following the syntactical, logical, or practical routes which connect them. But any sym-
bol which has more than an intersymbolic
meaning assigned to it by definition, goes back
to some authentic original. When one speaks
of the knowledge of "reality," one refers to
the recovery of this original by retracing the
trunk line of meaning; or to the detection and
naming of unfamiliar originals in the virgin
field of the hitherto unnoticed.

The unique and prior claim of this sort of
knowledge has been obscured by those who
claim its indubitable certainty. There is no
knowledge that *cannot* be doubted. An answer
is by definition the answer to a question, and
it is always *possible* to repeat the question. If
there be any absolute certainty it is to be
found not in the realm of immediacy, but
rather in the realm of logic, where there are
judgments that *may* not legitimately be
doubted; that is, the denial of which is self-
contradictory, or excluded by rules of pro-

cedure. The cognitive merit of immediate acquaintance does not lie in certainty, but in
insight. It is the knowledge that enables man,
the speaking animal, to avoid the self-inflicted
triviality of verbalism; it is the essentially
cognitive function as distinguished from that
skill, whether of word or hand, which "science"
represents; it provides the range of qualitative differences which constitute the ultimate
alternatives of taste and choice, and so save
life from the endless and unsatisfying linkage
of means to means.

The distinctive feature of James's empiricism is his insistence on this type of aesthetic,
as distinguished from either formal or practical, knowledge. This may seem a strange
characterization of a philosopher whose name
is identified in the public mind with pragmatism. But James himself has left no doubt of
the matter. Not only has he expressly and repeatedly stated that he considers his "radical
empiricism" to be more important than his
pragmatism; not only has he introduced the
pragmatic method as an accessory to immediate acquaintance or as a compensation for its
absence; but the delicate characterization of
experience—discoveries of data hitherto ignored, and vivid portrayals of the cosmic

scene—constitute the choicest fruits of his philosophical genius.

It would be a misunderstanding as mistaken as its opposite to suppose that because James was the champion of knowledge by acquaintance, his acceptance of "knowledge about" was an irrelevance which he borrowed from his times or from the philosophical tradition. He realized that actual experience is too limited to satisfy the purposes and claims of knowledge; that there are inevitable and significant questions whose answers carry beyond these limits; that these questions require a knowledge by which the content of the given is remembered and foreseen, or projected to a distance, or generalized and extended by analogy, in order that action may be oriented to all points of the spatio-temporal and social compass. Indeed he recognized that man's cognitive limitations are so ever-present and all-pervasive that the substitute for acquaintance is more characteristic than the original. Immediate knowledge is the best, but most human knowledge consists in making the best of a second best.

James is as insistent, then, as any modern scientist, that the great body of that which passes and serves as knowledge is indirect;

and consists of concepts of the object, and of operations directed to the object, rather than of an immediate envisagement of the object in its own intrinsic nature. He differs from the positivists in his insistence that acquaintance is also knowledge. He further insists that both conceptual and operational knowledge are dependent on knowledge by acquaintance. They are the best possible knowledge in the majority of cases, but they are, nonetheless, a second best. Concepts and operations are substitutes for immediacy, but they are qualified substitutes in so far as they are expectations of immediacy. Concepts are abstracted from experience; or, if they are pure conventions, they derive their meaning from their power, through association and agreement, to suggest experience. An operation may be substituted for any given object, when it would be appropriate to the presence of that object. Concepts and operations may be provisionally verified in terms of other concepts and operations; but their ultimate verification occurs only when an experience is as was expected, or when *what* was conceived or assumed in practice is realized in immediacy. He who frames a theoretical judgment that looks beyond the limits of his present experience, not only defines the objective reference of his judgment and commits himself in advance to the acceptance of its verdict, but entertains a specific expectation which is the condition of fulfillment or surprise. He is so set in advance that the moment of arrival brings a sense of "this is what I expected," or "this is not what I looked for." Thus a concept of tree, or method of dealing with tree, is conclusively verified only when it has prepared the thinker or agent for certain arboreal sensations and affections in which it terminates.

This duality of knowledge—this priority of acquaintance supplemented by knowledge about—obtains a broad and fundamental ex-emplification in the question of existence it-self. For certain sceptics, represented by San-tayana, a judgment of existence can never be verified. A general nature or "essence," which *might* exist can be immediately experienced, but its actually existing has to be taken on faith. Existence is always claimed and never found.[7] But in James's view it would be idle to use the word "existence" or to employ the idea, if it meant nothing in terms of experi-ence. In sense-perception there is a tang, a pungency, a vividness, a concreteness, a stub-bornness, with which it is possible to be ac-

7. Cf. Santayana, *Scepticism and Animal Faith* (1923), chaps. VII, VIII.

quainted. There is the object's present activity, not merely evoking the knower's adaptive countermeasures, but making itself felt. This is "what it is like to exist" and it is familiar to all who have lived among realities. As we have seen, immediate experience assumes for James a character which the term "sensation" can no longer adequately convey, least of all in that sense in which it is used to signify the atomic elements of psychological analysis. But sensory experience is still typical of existence in respect of that character of fullness, direct presence, and shock of externality which distinguishes it from thought, memory, and imagination.

Concerning existence there is also "knowledge about." In fact, most knowledge of existence is knowledge *about* existence. Such knowledge, for James, is verifiable in terms of ulterior experience, and in the customary absence of such experience is tested provisionally and indirectly by its consistency with other judgments. But James would think it strange that judgments of existence should appeal to ulterior experience, if that experience when actually present were unable to reveal existence. There would be no reason for supposing existence to lie outside of experience unless one knew *what it was* that lay outside. Unless men had some experience of what existence was, they could not miss it or declare it unattainable. What *is* that existence which Santayana relegates to "animal faith"? Faith in *what?* There is no meaningful answer to this question which does not imply that, however infrequent the encounter, existence is sometimes met face to face. Granting this, James would admit that the question of existence has in the great majority of cases to be decided in the *absence* of the immediacy which would constitute its only conclusive answer.

James's pragmatism is the form assumed in his empiricism by that "knowledge about," with which man is obliged to piece out his fragments of "acquaintance." There is a widespread confusion, for which James himself is in some measure responsible, between pragmatism and "fideism."[8] It is essential that this confusion be removed. Pragmatism is the application of practical principles to the theoretic process itself; fideism is the justification, on practical grounds, of overbelief—that is, of belief which lacks conclusive theoretic support. The one discovers the *practical* procedure of *theoretic* proof, the other affirms the practical right to believe in the absence of

8. Cf. below, chap. V.

such proof. Human knowledge may then be represented by three concentric areas. There is a nucleus of immediacy where existence and its characters are immediately present; beyond this lies an area of theoretic judgment in which belief is supported by reasons, embracing consistency with other judgments and verifiability in terms of experience; beyond this, finally, lies the area of faith, in which beliefs which transcend immediacy and are only negatively or partially supported by reasons are still justified on moral grounds.

Pragmatism, then, is the interpretation of the second of these areas, that of well-supported discursive or experimental knowledge. It stresses the act of initiative. Such knowledge is not a pure receptivity, but an attack, —inspired by a desire for truth or a state of discontent, and guided by a plan of campaign. It is a project framed or expectation entertained in advance, and then executed, so far as experience permits. It arises from an unpleasant situation, whether baffled curiosity or dissatisfying circumstance, and seeks relief by a trial of ideas. Its procedures will always be more or less relevant to that situation. It does not attack at random, but selects an objective which promises to remove its present quandary. It is, or may be, doubly interested:

interested in resolving doubt; and interested
in resolving *interesting* doubts, that is, doubts
which beset some concrete practical enterprise.

The idea whose provisional adoption is thus
motivated refers to an object of its own choosing, and its truth is to be judged relatively to
that object—to its *chosen* object. The idea or
the judgment in which it is affirmed must
somehow designate its object, point to it, or
lay out a route by which it may be found.
Knowledge by an idea must, in short, define
a direction which if prolonged would terminate in the object to which the idea's truth or
falsity is submitted. Knowledge "about" is so
constituted as to identify that which it is
about; its being "about" means that it moves
toward a certain destination; and that which
it is "about" is at the same time the arbiter of
its success and failure. Thus, if I frame a
judgment about the Washington Monument,
I choose so to direct my thoughts as to terminate in the Washington Monument, and he
who would confirm or reject them must meet
me there, and accept what is there revealed.
My own thinking prescribes both the locus of
relevance and the test of truth or error, and
my critic must follow my lead.

But these liberal concessions to the claims
of discursive and experimental knowledge be-

ing made by James the pragmatist, they are overruled at every point by James the radical empiricist. Discursive knowledge borrows its meanings and its truth from acquaintance. Action is incited by experience, and its success, so far as it has any theoretical function, lies in the satisfaction which it affords through paving the way to ulterior experience. Furthermore, the very processes of discursive and experimental knowledge, if they are anything at all, are known *for what they are*, in the cognitive experience. Thinking and experimenting take place; they are themselves composed of terms, relations, structures, and transitions that *make* them what they are; and these are known finally and definitively only to one who being a knower is directly acquainted with the intrinsic peculiarities of knowing.

CHAPTER III

THE METAPHYSICS OF EXPERIENCE

THE transition from James's empirical theory of knowledge to his metaphysics of experience is to be found in the thesis that even those terms, relations, and structures that constitute "knowledge about," and which are commonly contrasted with experience, lie themselves within its field, and are known by acquaintance. James does not neglect that type of knowledge which involves thinking and experiment. His pragmatism, as we have seen, makes ample provision for it. But things are what they are to him who is acquainted with them, and "knowledge about" is itself one of the things to which this formula applies. Knowledge *takes place*, and its nature is revealed in the experience of knowing. "Knowing about" the moon refers in the last analysis, by intent, if not by attainment, to a specific set of lunar data. But if, being a philosopher rather than an astronomer or poet, one is interested in the "knowing about" rather than in the moon, then by the same principle, there is a reference to *cognitive* data. These may not, like the moon, be visible, but they will fall within the range of some form of immediate awareness. There is a "feeling" of what "knowing about" is like, just as there is a seeing what the moon is like. And just as the moon *is* what it looks like, so "knowing about" *is* what it is "felt" to be.

In order that the conception of experience may be competent to embrace the structures and activities of knowledge it needs first to be enriched. This constitutes the psychological phase of James's philosophy of experience. It then becomes possible to bring within experience certain classic dualities—the dualities of self and not-self, of knower and known, and of idea and object, the terms of which, one or both, have in the traditional dualisms, been supposed to lie outside experience; or, if not outside, then, at any rate, upon a different plane of experience from sense and feeling. The next and crucial step in James's empiricism is to bring within experience the distinction between mind and body. In order that this may be done, it is necessary to "neutralize" experience; that is, free it from exclusive association with consciousness in order that it may embrace the physical world as well. For experience in this neutral sense James employed the term "phenomenon" in his earlier years, but in his later and definitive statement, he substituted the expression "pure experience." The last and culminating step is to identify experience—thus enriched and containing within itself the dualities of knowledge and of mind and body—with the metaphysical reality.

Let us, then, trace James's advancing empiricism through its psychological phase, including the psychology of knowledge, its phenomenalistic phase, and its final metaphysical phase. These three phases are represented by three important essays or lectures: "On Some Omissions of Introspective Psychology," published in 1884; "Does 'Consciousness' Exist?" published in 1904; and "The Continuity of Experience," published in 1909.

The first of these essays grew out of a lecture delivered by James in 1883 before the Concord School of Philosophy. It was written in the white heat of inspiration, and was judged by its author to be an "important contribution" to that psychology which, during the decade of the '80's, he was writing chapter by chapter. Most of it afterwards found a place in the *Principles of Psychology,* in the chapter entitled "The Stream of Thought." Both of these titles are significant. The term "omissions" suggests that James found in his examination of the immediate content of consciousness something that the less observant eyes of his predecessors had overlooked. His discoveries and descriptions were additive rather than reductive. The term "stream," like other fluid metaphors which he used in his later writings, suggests that aspect of continuous change which was to James the most concrete character of the given world.

There was a double reason why James's psychological studies should have enriched rather than reorganized the content of introspective psychology. In the first place, he felt that to confine psychology within any methodological strait-jacket might unwittingly exclude some datum or insight destined to do for psychology what Galileo's principle of acceleration and Lavoisier's molecular hypothesis had done for physics and chemistry. Psychology, he thought, was as yet in its early beginnings when liberality of outlook, fertility of suggestion, and hospitality to facts were more timely than an aping of the manners of science. He thought that psychology should have the courage to be itself—and keep close to the genius of mind undeterred by any taboos imposed by physics and physiology. Least of all did he think that the experimental psycho-physics of his day should be accepted as defining the limits of psychology. Had he known the psychology of today, he would have said, "The tent of psychology should be large enough to provide a place for the bohemian and clinical speculations of a Freud, or the rigorous physiological methods of a Lashley, or the bold theoretical generalizations of a Köhler, or the useful statistical technique of a Spearman. Only time will tell which of these, or whether any of these, will yield the master hypothesis which will give to psychology that explanatory and predictive power, that control of the forces of nature, which has been achieved by the older sciences." James's psychology was, therefore, by deliberate intent, and not by inadvertence, an omnibus psychology, in which any psychologist of today can find some of his affirmations and none of his negations. James did, it is true, seek to be in a sense "positivistic." But the positivism of James was almost the precise opposite of the doctrine which now passes by that name. Contemporary positivism closes all doors but one, while James's positivism opened all doors and kept them open. He welcomed all comers, even vagrants, who had anything to say about the human mind, and he made excursions himself into all regions of that subject-matter.

The booty which he gathered he left in more or less disorderly piles. He was a collector rather than an interior decorator.

There was a second reason why James increased the data of psychology instead of reducing them to systematic form. He was highly gifted in the art of describing consciousness. He had an extraordinary sensuous and introspective acuity. He could capture obscure feelings and fleeting impressions which slipped through the coarser nets of other observers. His genius lay not so much in tracing identities as in detecting differences. Few men, even poets, have had a greater capacity for noting and conveying by graphic description that quality *sui generis* which each moment of immediate experience possesses for itself.

This capacity shows itself throughout James's entire work. It was not accidental that he should have been a nativist in his view of the perception of space. He was reluctant to reduce distance to motor experience because he was so vividly aware of the unique characters of out-thereness, depth, or cavernousness, which, whatever their genesis, simply are not the same as any sensation, memory, or judgment of motion. Similarly, it was impossible for James to reduce time to mathematical and quasi-spatial schemata. Time was to

James the intrinsic quality of pastness, the all-at-once-ness of the immediate present, the about-to-be of the impending future, or the continuous transition from moment to moment. A further example is afforded by James's alertness to somatic sensations—his discriminating discernment of the organic components of experience supplied by muscles, tendons, joints, or by the circulatory and respiratory systems.

The "omissions" of which psychologists had been guilty were mainly due, James thought, to their failure to free themselves from the habits of practical common sense. This latter attitude selects what is "important" and passes over the rest. It dwells on objects, crucial events, and focal points, neglecting the passage from one of these to another. The practically habituated mind flies from perch to perch, and is aware of the perch rather than of the passage. This is James's famous distinction between transitive and substantive states, to which Charles Peirce proposed to give the more picturesque names of "winged" and "unwinged."[1] The discovery of James is that these transitive states, despite their obscurity, are none the less *there*, for the sensitive and practised eye. They are not only

1. Perry, *op. cit.*, II, 414.

there in themselves, but they qualify their *termini*—both the has-just-been and the soon-about-to-be.

The philosophical significance of this discovery does not lie in a mere accumulation of new introspective items, but in its giving a verifiable meaning to concepts which had hitherto been abstract and verbal. It may, I think, be said that James's works contain the most thoroughgoing attempt which has ever been made to carry all the terms of discourse back to the original data of sense, or to other immediately discriminated *qualia*. Like Whitehead, he suggested that "feelings" was the best term to employ for these originals.[2] "Sensation" is too narrowly associated with apprehension through recognized end-organs. "Thought," "ideas," and "representations," all of which have been used for this or a similar purpose, are too closely associated with the processes of the intellect. If the term "feelings" is used, this term also must be freed from its own characteristic limitations, its exclusive association, namely, with affective or emotional states. The term must be used in a sense that makes it natural to speak of a "feel-

2. A. N. Whitehead, *Process and Reality* (1929), pp. 65–66.

ing of relation," or a "feeling of identity," or
a "feeling of drink-after-thirst," or a "feeling
of pastness and futurity." It is the apprehension of the *in-itselfness* of some root character, discriminable from all others, requiring a
name of its own, and evoking the comment, "I
see what it is," from minds possessed of the
appropriate sensibilities and directed to the
right context. The following is an instructive
statement of James's radically empirical view
of meaning:

It boots not to say that our sensations are falli-
ble. They are indeed; but to see the thermometer
contradict us when we say "it is cold" does not
abolish cold as a specific nature from the universe. Cold is in the arctic circle if not here.
Even so, to feel that our train is moving when
the train beside our window moves, to see the
moon through a telescope come twice as near, or
to see two pictures as one solid when we look
through a stereoscope at them, leaves motion,
nearness, and solidity still in being—if not here,
yet each in its proper seat elsewhere. And wherever the seat of real causality *is*, as ultimately
known "for true" (in nerve-processes, if you
will, that cause our feelings of activity as well as
the movements which these seem to prompt), a
philosophy of pure experience can consider the
real causation as no other *nature* of thing than

that which even in our most erroneous experiences appears to be at work.[3]

The philosophical fruitfulness of James's enrichment of conscious experience lay especially in its giving empirical meaning to that relation of "subject" and "object" which under different names and aspects was in James's day considered to be the distinctive feature of knowing. The subject, in thinking, at least, if not in perceiving, is active; the object passive. The subject is the self, named by the first personal pronoun, the object is not-self. The subject sets in orderly arrangement the raw material provided by the object. The subject frames ideas which represent or refer to the object. Now in James's day it was customary among philosophers to consider the knowing subject together with its peculiar relations to its object, as lying outside the manifold of conscious experience. Being inherently and inescapably subjective, it could never change places with its object; attempt to make an object of it, and it will instantly identify itself with the subject of that new object. Look at it, and it becomes the looker, feel it and it becomes the feeler, think it and it becomes the

3. "The Experience of Activity," *Essays in Radical Empiricism* (1912), pp. 182–183.

thinker. It was the "from" or the "for," never
the "at" or the "to" of knowing. It hovered in
the air above the field of objects, and from its
detached station directed itself now to one and
now to another; or by concerning itself with
several objects at once, brought them into
those interrelations which compose the order
of nature. In itself it was elusive to the knowing eye; always so far in the foreground that
it found no place in the landscape.

But to an empiricist the subject, in all its
guises and roles, must if it has any meaning
be identified with some element of experience.
James's empirical forerunners of the British
school were not good enough empiricists to
suit James. The object remained transempiri-
cal in the physical substance of Locke; the
subject in the spiritual substance of Berkeley.
Hume was driven to scepticism by the ghost
of substances to which he could give no meaning. For James there was no residual subjectivity or objectivity whose authentic original
was not presented; and since both subject and
object and their characteristic relations *were*
presented, there was no occasion for despair.

James found that an important step toward
this thoroughgoing empiricism had been taken
by Locke, who with characteristic moderation
had failed to realize its full consequences. Per-

sonal identity, Locke had said, is that identity of which we are conscious, the experience that "makes a man be himself to himself." To James, "the importance of Locke's doctrine lay in this, that he eliminated 'substantial' identity as transcendental and unimportant, and made of 'personal' identity (the only practically important sort) a directly verifiable empirical phenomenon. Where not actually experienced, it *is* not."[4] The gravity of this step lies in the fact that the cognitive subject, the knowing self, takes its place within the field of its own knowing. The knower takes its place among the known. Berkeley, though he had brought the physical object wholly within the perceptual field, had still reserved a place apart for the spiritual perceiver, of whose acts it was possible to possess an intuitive awareness which he termed a "notion," but which never mingled with the vulgar herd of percepts. In James, the personal subject loses all of its special privileges. It must submit to the common test. If it is there at all it must give evidence of its existence, and this evidence furnishes, so far as it goes, the only clue to its nature and character.

4. John Locke, *An Essay Concerning Human Understanding* (1853), Book II, chap. XXVII, 10; James, "Person and Personality," *Johnson's Universal Cyclopaedia* (1895), VI, 539.

This does not mean that the duality of self and not-self is denied or disregarded. On the contrary James's fear of verbal entities introduced *ad hoc* leads him to multiply significant meanings. Instead of one self there are many selves—empirical, material, social, and spiritual. Personal identity is not rejected, but elaborated into feelings of activity, of warmth and intimacy, or of bodily states. The cognitive subject is not omitted, but is construed as the "judging thought" which, binding together the past with the present, unites the plurality of experiences, appropriates them, and transmits them to its successor.[5] The effect of abolishing fictions is thus the enrichment and not the impoverishment of concepts.

It may be objected that when the person, self, and subject are thus discovered in experience they are "objectified," and imply another mental agent which, being their discoverer, cannot be discovered among them. But when the new subject in turn is reflected upon, it reveals the same nature as the old. Beyond a certain point the repetition of this operation of reflective self-awareness yields nothing new, but only corroborates its previous findings, just as one can conclude after

5. Cf. James, *The Principles of Psychology* (1890), I 333–338.

several turnings what, if anything, is behind one's back.

James's reduction of subject and object to the "stream of thought" had an important bearing on the traditional duality between form and content. The most notable "omissions" of introspective psychology which James had sought to restore were those relationships which give form or order to the objective world. A faulty introspection had pulverized experience into elements. Since it was impossible to deny that these elements stood in relations of some sort, since they were at least multiple, contiguous, and successive, and since introspection failed to find relations *among* them, it was necessary to assume these relations to be somehow introduced by the observing subject itself. Since, furthermore, the assumed relations gave the elements their arrangement and structure, and thus constituted nature or cosmos, they were, philosophically speaking, the most fundamental feature of the system. They supplied both its dynamics and its architectural form. They were either tacitly assumed as by Hume, in his principle of association; or, "deduced" as necessary "categories," after the manner of Kant and his school. In either case their affirmation was in violation of that fundamental maxim of empiricism which prohibits the introduction of terms not traceable to data of experience.

James proposed to return again to original experience as it stood before introspective analysis had divided it into elements. Looking more carefully, one finds that the connective tissue was there all the time. The elements have been abstracted from a context. Restoring the context one finds the elements embedded in a matrix of relationships. Avoiding the natural preoccupation with focal points and substantive nuclei, one can detect not only distinct qualities and things, but spatial and temporal juxtaposition, causal nexus, identity, difference and contrast, and a hundred other relations; many of them represented in speech by conjunctions, prepositions, punctuation, and syntactical inflections, others having no linguistic equivalents at all because irrelevant to the purposes of ordinary discourse.

The second traditional duality which James's revised empiricism reduces to the common terms of experience is that between idea and object. In the case of acquaintance, the idea becomes confluent with its object. Even here the presentation may be called an idea or "thought," if one wishes to stress "the omnipresence of cognition"; for a unit of conscious experience is always an experience of something, in the sense of its content as distinguished from the act of apprehension. But in thoughts or ideas having a reference beyond the present experience we remark two objectivities, one internal and one external. The internal object is the experience of reference itself. My thought that "Columbus discovered America in 1492" has a specific internal complexity of deliverance embracing some shading of "Columbus," "America," "discovery," and "1492"—"with every word fringed and the whole sentence bathed in that original halo of obscure relations, which, like an horizon, then spread about its meaning."[6] This objectivity *occurs*, in the now-present experience. But there is also an objectivity *to* which the thought refers. Over and above its present *meaningfulness*, consisting in the irradiation of the fringe within the circle of its horizon, there is also its *meant*, the non-present experience which is defined by the fringe's orientation. This ulterior and contingent experience consists, for example, of Columbus' experience of America in 1492, or, perhaps, his alibi. In the case of the past such an ulterior perception cannot be reached, and the thought's reference can be corroborated only indirectly.

6. *Idem*, I, 275–276.

In other cases, such as, "There is a coat in the closet," the ulterior perception can follow upon the thought, by a smooth transition along lines of felt tendency, and without stepping out of the stream of experience. Interpreted on this analogy, even the ulterior objective meanings which remain transcendent, become a set of experiences differing not in any radical sense, but only in their accidental inaccessibility. As distant, hypothetical, or possible experiences, they are of the same nature, and lie in the same field, as the present experience. Thus while James does not deny the distinction between idea and object, but on the contrary subjects it to a most refined analysis, he so restates the duality as to bring it wholly, both its terms and their characteristic interrelations, within the conscious continuum or its prolongation.

So far James claimed no more than an enrichment of the content of consciousness—a supplementation of the data accessible to introspection, and capable of description. For the limited "scientific" purposes of psychology he still assumed an ulterior physical object beyond consciousness, as well as the brain and other physiological mechanisms which he employed for purposes of explanation. But he had long entertained a more radical view in which these basic structures themselves were radically reconstructed. In 1904 in a series of articles posthumously published under the title of *Essays in Radical Empiricism*, he boldly proclaimed a revolutionary view, which he said he had harbored for twenty years, that is, from the time when he had first formulated the psychological doctrine which we have just examined. James himself spoke of this second stage of his developing empiricism as "methodological":

The principle of pure experience is also a methodical postulate. Nothing shall be admitted as fact, it says, except what can be experienced at some definite time by some experient; and for every feature of fact ever so experienced, a definite place must be found somewhere in the final system of reality. In other words: Everything real must be experienceable somewhere, and every kind of thing experienced must somewhere be real."[7]

But this statement does not give sufficient emphasis to the crux of James's "radicalism." To insist that every fact shall be identified with data of experience still leaves open the question of experience itself, and is quite con-

7. "The Experience of Activity," *Essays in Radical Empiricism* (1912), p. 160.

sistent with the assumption that experience is identical with consciousness. If one submits consciousness itself to the same empirical criterion, and affirms that the difference between mind and body itself is an experienced difference, then it is clear that experience must be assigned a more extended meaning than consciousness. The radicalism of James's "radical" empiricism, then, lies in its application to consciousness, and requires a new term such as "phenomenon" or "*pure* experience," which shall not be confused with consciousness, but shall constitute a more inclusive manifold within which consciousness itself shall be distinguished and explained.

In putting the question, "Does 'Consciousness' Exist?" James did not, of course, mean to doubt the existence of consciousness in *some* sense, but only to reject that traditional sense which he had himself provisionally accepted. Hitherto it had been assumed that consciousness and experience were the same thing. The knowing subject and the known object had both been reduced to experience, but both fell within consciousness: both were made of the same conscious stuff, or embraced within the same conscious container. But what does this word "conscious" mean when "subject," "self," and "knower" are all embraced within it? As a good empiricist James was bound to look for its meaning in experience, and find there some specific content for which it was the name. Applying this method strictly he found that, construed as an aboriginal stuff or all-enveloping container, it had *no* meaning. Searching for a meaning in terms of experience he found consciousness, like the knowing subject, to consist in a peculiar relationship among the terms of experience. Thus while it means nothing to say that yellow is made of conscious stuff, or is contained within a conscious receptacle, it does mean something to say that when the yellow of the rose is connected by expectation with other sensory data, such as fragrance, or with melancholy memories or romantic hopes, then these elements *compose* consciousness. They constitute a peculiar togetherness whose structural characteristic is consciousness, though the components are in themselves not conscious at all. The effect of this analysis was to introduce a more original congeries of elements which, being intrinsically non-conscious, might in specific types of combination constitute not only consciousness, but also other orders of being, such as the physical world.

The new meaning of consciousness may be

illustrated by its application to the notion of objectivity. There are, as we have seen, dualities of subject and object, knower and known, self and not-self, form and content, idea and object, which James by his recognition of "transitive states" had assimilated to the stream of consciousness, actual and possible. There is, however, a further duality which now for the first time receives explicit empirical interpretation, that, namely, between the knowing mind and the "external" world. It is characteristic of knowledge of the physical world not only that it institutes an object-over-against-subject relation within consciousness, but that the object in this relation has a different *ontological* status from that of the subject. It has not only its cognitive objectivity, but also its metaphysical objectivity, in the sense of belonging to another order than that mentality into which, through being known, it is introduced. Physical knowledge is an act by which a mind somehow reaches beyond mind.

James can now provide for this further objectivity not by the agnostic appeal to an externality beyond experience, but by conceiving that the physical order and the mental order overlap in common phenomena or pure experience. The mind literally embraces, incorporates into itself, elements which "belong" at the same time to the physical world. The Cartesian dualism of substance is superseded by a difference of relations or functions among "neutral" terms.

As to details, James's view can only be regarded as tentative—as adopting a type of solution not yet definitively formulated. The mental relationship is distinguished negatively from the physical, through lack of dynamic efficacy. Thus fire does not burn that with which it is brought into a merely mental juxtaposition. If one turns to the positive characteristics of the mental order, there are at least three which appear in James's account. There is the process of reflection, in which a first experience is corrected and transcended by a supervening experience. There is the cognitive reference in which one experience "points to" an ulterior experience. Finally, there is the factor of interested selectivity, so conspicuous throughout all of James's descriptions of mind. In all of these cases consciousness is a peculiar structure of elements, none of which in itself is intrinsically conscious or mental or personal. James also referred to certain organic sensations of a peculiarly intimate sort—breathing, for example, or sensations in the head, as providing a specific datum of subjectivity.[8] There is no definitive and systematic conclusion of this matter. But the principle is clear, namely, that both subjectivity in the mental sense and objectivity in the physical sense are particular modes of experience in the "pure" or "phenomenal" sense.

There is a similar inconclusiveness as regards the conception of experience itself, in its "pure" or phenomenalistic significance. This second phase of James's philosophy of experience is primarily an analysis, a *reduction* of the bodily and mental worlds to the same original components. "Pure experience" is the severalty of these identical components —to speak of the "world" of pure experience is as yet premature. Its "purity" means that the components are taken on a primitive level, where they are not yet qualified as physical or mental. Pure experience is "the instant field of the present," detached from its context or functional role. It is the "potentiality" of the mental and physical. It is a class name for a set of data which have no general "stuff"—"a

8. Cf. "Does 'Consciousness' Exist?" *Essays in Radical Empiricism* (1912), p. 37; *Principles of Psychology* (1890), I, 299–306.

collective name for all . . . sensible natures,"
such as "space, . . . intensity, . . . flatness,
brownness, heaviness."[9]

If consciousness is a special relation of
these elements, then the other relations must
be non-conscious. If pure experience is indeed
neutral, then it is capable of being actual in
the absence of that peculiar modification of
itself which constitutes consciousness. But
James frequently writes as though experience
and conscious experience were the same thing.
Consider, for example, the following passage
so characteristically Jamesian in its pictorial
quality and descriptive skill:

Prima facie, if you should liken the universe of
absolute idealism to an aquarium, a crystal
globe in which goldfish are swimming, you would
have to compare the empiricist universe to something more like one of those dried human heads
with which the Dyaks of Borneo deck their
lodges. The skull forms a solid nucleus; but innumerable feathers, leaves, strings, beads, and
loose appendices of every description float and
dangle from it, and, save that they terminate in
it, seem to have nothing to do with one another.
Even so my experiences and yours float and dangle, terminating, it is true, in a nucleus of com-

9. "Does 'Consciousness' Exist?" *Essays in Radical
Empiricism* (1912), pp. 23, 26–27.

mon perception, but for the most part out of sight and irrelevant and unimaginable to one another. . . . The distant parts of the physical world are at all times absent from us, and form conceptual objects merely, into the perceptual reality of which our life inserts itself at points discrete and relatively rare. Round their several objective nuclei, partly shared and common and partly discrete, of the real physical world, innumerable thinkers, pursuing their several lines of physically true cogitation, trace paths that intersect one another only at discontinuous perceptual points, and the rest of the time are quite incongruent; and around all the nuclei of shared "reality," as around the Dyak's head of my late metaphor, floats the vast cloud of experiences that are wholly subjective, that are non-substitutional, that find not even an eventual ending for themselves in the perceptual world—the mere day-dreams and joys and sufferings and wishes of the individual minds.[10]

But this is the empiricist universe only in the limited sense of the world consciously experienced by human subjects. To constitute the universe in the neutral sense it would have to be filled out with the "perceptual reality" of that "distant physical world" and of those other regions into which our life does not and

10. "A World of Pure Experience," *Essays in Radical Empiricism* (1912), pp. 46–47, 65–66.

cannot enter. Such a world would still contain James's Dyak world—but its features would be extended and multiplied beyond the accidental limitations of human consciousness.

It is regrettable that James was not more persistently and stubbornly consistent in his own radicalism. If experience is to have the physical and metaphysical scope which he attributed to it, it must be boldly emancipated from all conscious or mental implications. I assume, then, arguing James against himself, that in the phenomenalistic phase of his development he introduced pure experience as the aboriginal form of being, embracing consciousness, together with non-conscious or non-mental forms of being, such as bodies. This I take to be the basic conception of that final metaphysic to which we now turn.

In the volume entitled *A Pluralistic Universe* James was emboldened, in partnership with Bergson, to elevate "experience"—this same immediacy which he had enriched by introspective discovery, this same qualitative manifold into which he had resolved the physical and mental orders—to the rank of the ultimate reality. To serve a metaphysical purpose it is not sufficient that experience should be a stream of subjectivity dependent on a brain, and intermediate between an inner soul and an outer object, or a class name for miscellaneous phenomenal entities more primitive than mind or body. It must have a form of its own, enabling it to exist in its own terms. It must embrace both mind and body, and all other modes of existence, not as regards their abstract components merely, but as regards their forms of relatedness. And it must possess the maximum of concreteness as well as of universality. In this phase of his philosophy of experience James is indubitably attempting a highest synthesis, in which the physiognomy of the universe shall stand forth in its own native character.

"The deeper features of reality," says James, "are found only in perceptual experience."[11] But these deeper features are not the *obvious* features of perception. Let me cite a passage in which James identifies "reality" with a peculiarly adequate experience—not with the careless glance of ordinary life, but with the difficult and rare realization of an insight which is always near at hand:

There is something in life, as one feels its presence, that seems to defy all the possible resources of phraseology. . . . Life defies our phrases,

11. *Some Problems of Philosophy* (1911), p. 97.

not only because it is infinitely continuous and
subtle and shaded, whilst our verbal terms are
discrete, rude and few; but because of a deeper
discrepancy still. Our words come together lean-
ing on each other laterally for support, in chains
and propositions, and there is never a proposi-
tion that does not require other propositions
after it, to amplify it, restrict it, or in some way
save it from the falsity by defect or excess which
it contains. . . . Life, too, in one sense, stum-
bles over its own feet in a similar way; for its
earlier moments plunge ceaselessly into later
ones which reinterpret and correct them. Yet
there is something else than this in life, something entirely unparalleled by anything in verbal thought. The living moments—some living
moments, at any rate—have somewhat of absolute that needs no lateral support. Their meaning seems to well up from out of their very cen-
tre, in a way impossible verbally to describe. If
you take a disk painted with a concentric spiral
pattern, and make it revolve, it will seem to be
growing continuously and indefinitely, and yet
to take in nothing from without; and to remain,
if you pay attention to its actual size, always of
the *same* size. Something as paradoxical as this
lies in every present moment of life.[12]

12. Original paragraph which James wrote for the
opening of the Gifford Lectures subsequently published
under the title, *The Varieties of Religious Experience,*
quoted by Perry, *op. cit.,* II, 328.

These moments, as I understand them, are the moments of integration, when experience is revealed in that respect in which it *"is self-containing and leans on nothing."*[13] I shall now attempt to enumerate these "deeper features," and present reality as it revealed itself to James's metaphysical genius.

Certain of the characteristics of reality are already implied in identifying it with experience. It will have that character of qualitative specificity and diversity which is the great and unique contribution of the senses and feelings. It will consist of color, tone, hardness, sweetness and all the innumerable and nameless nuances by which such qualities are shaded, mixed, and related. In the next place, it will possess that vividness or pungency by which the sensory and affective life is distinguished from the paler and flatter tone of ideas and memories. It will, of course, embrace ideas and memories, but in that living aspect which is evident when they in turn are presented in their own right, and not merely represented by, or serving as representations of, some other entity.

A further character is implied in the gradual conquest of human knowledge, which,

13. "The Essence of Humanism," *Essays in Radical Empiricism,* p. 193.

starting with ignorance, approaches reality through a series of partial glimpses. Reality is unfolded by thought and is always more than any of its unfoldings. What is commonly *thought* to be real is a selection, dictated by some interest or defined by some point of view. At the same time that this selectiveness is recognized, it is also evident that a greater fullness envelops and contains the selection. To select is to select *from*, which implies not only a residuum excluded from the selection, but a togetherness of the included and the excluded in the original plenum. This plenum must not only contain the selections made from it, but must be so constituted as to permit of its being selectively divided. It must be a field of eligibility. As such it is a world suitable to the exercise of freedom.

The effort of metaphysics is to reconstitute this undivided field of choice. Being aware of the selectiveness of action and thought the metaphysician will discount their effects. This he will be enabled to do in proportion as he is aware of the principle of his selection. He will be able to unmake in the degree to which he understands the making. But the act of selection will not have been wasted, even for theoretical purposes. The reservoir of experience will be such as to yield to selection, and such as to yield this or that particular selection. It will thereafter be known not only as that *from* which selection has been made, but as that from which this *particular* selection has been made, and which must in some sense have contained the selection before it was made. If I use the expression "in some sense," it is not in order to avoid a downright affirmation, but to suggest that the sense in which a reservoir contains what is selected from it, is not so simple as is ordinarily supposed. All selection, even discrimination and abstraction, is transformation. The reservoir is such that if a certain kind of selective act is applied to it a certain excerpt will result. The act can be repeated with the same result, and the process can be reversed. In the case of conscious experience, or cognition, however, the act of synthetic restoration does not cancel the act of analysis. As in sensory discrimination, the element selected can thereafter be noted along with its context. The excerpt once made is thereafter present as an enrichment of the concrete immediacy. After analysis the mind is enabled to apprehend a greater volume of experience, as the instruments of an orchestra first noted separately can then be heard together. The aim of metaphysics is to profit by selective attention so that the differentiated features may be embodied in a more adequate and inclusive synthesis.

Closely related to this voluminous and plenary character of the metaphysical experience is its quality of originality, a generalization of James's psychological nativism. Reality is the shameless, unreconstructed, uncensored primitiveness. That this is close to the heart of James's temperamental insight is proved by the revealing paragraph which he wrote in a notebook of 1902, in which he confessed his antipathy to what is artificial and schematic. Systems are not only limited and partial, but they have a sharpness of boundary, a groomed and doctored character which is opposed to reality in its natural state:

What, on pragmatist terms, does "nature itself" signify? To my mind it signifies the non-artificial; the artificial having certain definite aesthetic characteristics which I dislike, and can only apperceive in others as matters of personal taste,—to me bad taste. All neat schematisms with permanent and absolute distinctions, classifications with absolute pretensions, systems with pigeon-holes, etc., have this character.[14]

The real world signifies inexhaustible fecundity. The universe is not an order, but that

14. Perry, *op. cit.*, II, 700; also cf. above, p. 26, note 23.

of which every type of order is only a limited aspect. A universe conceived as a pure Eleatic being, or as a Spinozistic substance of quasi-mathematical necessity, or as a self-conscious mind, or as a moral will, or as a mechanics of matter, would in James's view be the mere extension of an abstraction too thin to carry any adequate impression of aboriginal plenitude. Neither abstractionism nor organism will suit James's metaphysics. His universe is a universe by virtue of its omitting nothing, by virtue of its indeterminate immensity and complexity, its unanalyzed ingredients, its unplumbed depths, its passage beyond every horizon, and not by virtue of any architecture, or structural delimitation, whether logical, aesthetic, or moral.

Limitation, instead of being, as with the Greeks, a dignity, is for James a narrowing and impoverishment. Bergson has with evident sympathy called attention to this feature of James's metaphysics. "La réalité, telle que James la voit, est redondante et surabondante."[15] This reality that overflows all bounds and fills all interstices, providing a perpetual residuum which escapes even the most meticulous analysis and the most comprehensive gen-

15. Henri Bergson, *La Pensée et le mouvant* (1934), p. 268.

eralizations—this reality that runs off the palms and slips through the fingers of the most dexterous thought—is a companion notion to that of selectiveness. For James, as for Bergson, both thought and action are selective—both being manifestations, perhaps, of the same selective interest. But selection always implies omission, something excluded as well as something included. He who is unaware of the selective motive which governs him will take his selection to be exhaustive; while to be aware of it is to transcend its limits. Thus James and Bergson, who see the omnipresence of selection, and in that sense emphasize it, are peculiarly competent to introduce the necessary corrective or compensation.

In the light of these considerations, then, James's world of experience is that fullness of reality which embraces the excerpts of thought and action, together with the selective activity and motive itself, and the context in which the excerpt is naturally or originally immersed. The world is a selection in the making, amidst a superabundance of the unselected.

A further feature of James's universe is its continuity. He describes the metaphysics set forth in *A Pluralistic Universe* as "my attempt at a synechistic solution of the one *vs.* the many problem"; or as "the Bergsonian

separation of the immediate flux as containing all life's dynamisms, from our conceptual
treatment of it as only a map for practical
purposes."[16]

Continuity has to be reconciled with the
discreteness of those moments of experience
which grasp change "all at once," and thus
embrace it within themselves; and with that
distinctness which is implied not only in
James's emphasis on qualitative uniqueness,
but in his moral individualism. He does not
evade this difficulty, but proposes to overcome
it by the notion of a manifold of overlapping
particulars. In its temporal application this
means that every moment is both retrospec-
tive and prospective as well as present. As moments succeed one another they take over, or,
to use Whitehead's term, "inherit," from one
another. Individuals are unique and yet they
have a community of experience. Every exist-
ent element has its own discriminable character, and yet it is soaked as well as bathed in
the context in which it is immersed; and there
is a chemistry by which each synthesis possesses a uniqueness of its own.

James made much, especially in the last of

16. Perry, *op. cit.* (1935), II, 651; cf. also II, 411, 656.
"Synechism" is Charles Peirce's term for a theory which
affirms continuity.

his written works, of the distinction between concepts and percepts. This distinction presents a problem for metaphysics which it does not present for a mere theory of knowledge. The latter can distinguish between the concept as an instrument and the reality or datum to which it applies. Metaphysics, on the other hand, must bring them into the same world. The comparative unreality of concepts must somehow be reconciled with the fact that *there are* concepts. Similarly the field of their application must be so constituted as to permit of their application. If we say that the authentic features of reality are revealed in perceptual experience, we must explain how such a reality can harbor that which is antithetical to percepts, namely, concepts; and how percepts are conceivable, that is, lend themselves to conceptual treatment. There is a further difficulty in the fact, repeatedly admitted by James, that concepts have a certain objectivity of their own which makes it possible to visit and explore them on their own premises. James, as well as Bergson, faced these difficulties.

James's solution is here, as elsewhere, a suggestion rather than an elaborated explanation. The essence of it lies in regarding concepts as abstractions, cuts, excerpts, taken from the plenum of reality by an interested act of selection. They present reality in some partial aspect suitable to action, and discourse, or serve as a substitute for the fuller experience when this is unattainable. Being selected they are not removed or set apart in any spatial or ontological sense. They are not entities by themselves, or duplications of perception. They are not "really" separate. They are separate only in the sense of being distinguished,—the selective act uses them and neglects the rest, but the rest is there. They are real in their concreteness, at the same time that they are unreal when "taken" by themselves. Nevertheless, being so "taken," they can be inspected, compared, and interrelated so as to give rise to a type of knowledge which, though not a knowledge of reality in the full metaphysical sense, does envisage what may be termed "an ideal world."

James's image of the stream connotes fluidity as well as continuity. He is a modern Heraclitean in his unqualified acceptance of the all-permeating character of change. But while James's last word is Heraclitean, he does not neglect the consideration which gives Eleaticism its right to be heard. Fixed meanings do occur. To cut an element from the stream of change is to divest it of the character of change which it derives from its presence in the stream. It is not "really" unchanging, for "really" refers to its native habitat. It is framed in by the act of selection so that its character of change is hidden from view. This act may be repeated. One may mean the same, as often as convenient, in repeated acts of abstractive contemplation.

James's "pluralism" and "indeterminism" lie in his viewing the world as a field in which determination is proportional to proximity, and in which forces and influences are centrifugal rather than centripetal. One does not explain parts as the internal differentiation of a prior whole, but the whole as the resultant of the action of the parts. What unity there is is of the "strung-along type, the type of continuity, contiguity, or concatenation."[17] Moments of existence lying close together interpenetrate and have a relatively high measure of mutual impregnation. Forces become attenuated by distance and mixed by indirection. The same illimitable fecundity which characterizes the world in its internal composition also characterizes its history. It is, no doubt, a world in which the expected happens, in which predictions are possible—possible to an increasing extent. But it still remains at

17. *A Pluralistic Universe* (1909), p. 325.

bottom a world which is full of surprises—in which laws are outmoded, in which new laws have to be framed, and which is always exceeding the limits of any preconceived scheme. While it is thus *both* predictable and unpredictable, James would say that the latter is its deeper character. Human convenience and habit are on the side of law and order. But this is perhaps the human prepossession which has done most to blind philosophers. It is the philosophical prejudice *par excellence*. And it might be added that for James a more or less unpredictable world, reasonably well behaved but retaining a dash of primeval naughtiness, was not only the most authentic revelation of experience, but also the most interesting and exciting world in which to live.

What shall one say of the validity of a metaphysical generalization such as that of James? Santayana conceives of James as a romanticist. According to this critic, while his philosophy is an interesting expression, perhaps the most genuine expression, of the American soul—it is idle to speak of it as true or false, or even as profitable or unprofitable.[18]

18. Cf. George Santayana, "The Genteel Tradition in American Philosophy," *Winds of Doctrine* (1913), pp. 210–211.

Now the philosophy of experience claims to be empirical—claims to *discover* this sensuous and qualitative character, this selectiveness, this amplitude, this continuity, pluralism and novelty—as the evident characters of that world in which man lives. The description may be false, but if so the way to disprove it is to look at what is being described and to undertake a better description. In any case, nothing could be further from the truth than to suppose that James was romantic in any sense of extemporization, or of lawless fancy. To his mind the task of the empirical metaphysician was peculiarly difficult:

Something forever exceeds, escapes from statement, withdraws from definition, must be glimpsed and felt, not told. No one knows this like your genuine professor of philosophy. For what glimmers and twinkles like a bird's wing in the sunshine it is his business to snatch and fix.[19]

I submit that there is discipline, meticulousness, and intellectual integrity as well as rare power of discrimination and of description in this "snatching and fixing" of what only "glimmers and twinkles."

Nor can it be justly said that James played fast and loose with logic. He did not, it is

19. Quoted in Perry, *op. cit.*, II, 329.

true, attempt to erect a deductive system. He
did, it is true, renounce logic at a certain crisis
in his thought, when he believed that the traditional and authoritative logic of his day
compelled him to deny the plain deliverance
of his experience. It is also true that he was,
or believed himself to be, relatively incompe-
tent in the processes of formal and symbolic
thinking. On the other hand, no man has ever
made a more heroic struggle to think consistently, or to abide by the consequences of his
own affirmations. His very abandonment of
logic was in fact the adoption of another way
of thinking which is equally deserving of the
name of logic. The crux of the difficulty for
James lay in the concept of identity. He could
not accept a logic which forbade that differences should be predicated of the same; and
which denied that one entity could be in some
sense both identical and non-identical with another. The first of these paradoxes he escaped
by treating certain predicates as relations, as
when he said that the same may be both mental, physical, or neither, when taken in a first
relation, a second relation, or in no relation.
The second paradox he escaped by taking the
concrete entity as an integrated complex
which by overlapping another could be both
identical with that other as regards their com-

munity, and also non-identical as regards their individualities and private remainders.

Of one thing, as an unashamed and stubborn empiricist, James was sure, namely, that the must-be's or cannot-be's of logic must in the end yield to the facts of experience. If there is such a disagreement, then logic must give way. For it is the function of logic to be an aid to description—to contribute definite conceptual alternatives from which experience can choose. The finding of direct experience pronounces the last word.

An empiricism such as that of James may fairly claim not only to provide an intimate revelation of original facts, but to heal the breach between facts and values. The realm of value is the realm of choice and of feeling. These attitudes themselves, and their emotional reverberations, are immediacies of experience; and in the end, where value is final and intrinsic, they are evoked by the immediacies of experience. To the normal man who likes, enjoys, hopes, resolves, and appreciates, even to the abstract thinker when he is thus a normal man, or when he relishes his own abstractions, James's world is the "real" world: the world of action and the world of those enjoyments by which action is motivated and justified.

The philosophy of immediate experience finds a reverberation or confirmation among the arts, both literary and visual, in certain tendencies which we are pleased to consider modern. Whether there is here some indirect and unconscious influence, or only a simultaneous manifestation of the same *Zeitgeist* I cannot say. But there is an undoubted relation—instructive for exposition, even if it throws no light on the explanation of origins. Modern biography is disposed to render a man's life in terms of self-feeling; in terms of the subject's own experience, rather than in terms of external events. The idea of the "stream of consciousness" as represented by James Joyce, by Proust, and by their critics, embraces a conception of memory which is Bergsonian and Freudian, rather than Jamesian, in its affiliations: Bergsonian in its antithesis between the pure memory which evokes the plenum of past images, and the selective memory which, omitting all that is irrelevant, applies the past experience to the present action; Freudian in its notion that the memories recalled by free association reveal the hidden springs of action which are otherwise suppressed or distorted by scruple. There remain conceptions that are unmistakably Jamesian—though often Bergsonian as well. First among these is the continuity, the "déroulement ininterrompu," of conscious experience, when released from the conceptual schematisms imposed by naturalistic assumptions, or by the logic of common sense. Judged by these norms the full immediacy is incoherent:

Tout ce qu'il traverse dans la tête d'un individu, prodigieusement quotidien, d'idées, de souvenirs, de vantardises, et avec la minutie et le désordre d'évocation qui peut y régner, tout ce que la pensée d'un homme voit surgir, à toute minute, de velléités ridicules, tout cela est rendu avec les boursouflures de l'orgueil et de la bêtise collective et particulière que chacun de nous a en partage. Toute cette meute de pensées s'agite en nous, sans repos, comme un troupeau apocalyptique; troupeau aux courses énergumènes. Elucubrations incohérentes, déformations hilarantes, visions démonologiques, prouesses scatologiques, bouffées de poésie, telle est la bacchanale silencieuse et rapide qui se profile au fond de nous, comme au fond de la caverne de Platon se profilaient des ombres, mais moins inquiétantes.

To depict this continuity requires a

prodigieuse délicatesse à saisir toutes les nuances de l'esprit, à mêler le monde extérieur au monde intérieur, à noter en petites phrases courtes, vives et légères, le perpétuel travail de volition, de réflexion, d'inconscient, qui tisse et détisse sans fin des toiles presque indistinctes au fond de notre âme.

A second Jamesian feature of this literary stream of consciousness is the blend of thought, perception and feeling: "Toutes les idées et images, sensations physiologiques et affectives . . . qui successivement ou simultanément se développent en un cerveau." The sensory field is qualified not only by its own proper hues, but by a foreground of feeling. The description is not of objects and of actions, but of the experience of objects and actions, as this is enjoyed by a subject or participant. The same notion is advanced by those painters who would depict not the object as understood, divided from foreground and context by practical or theoretical faculties of selection, but the consciousness of the painter himself in the presence of the object.[20]

Aldous Huxley, in an exposition of D. H. Lawrence, reverses the metaphor of Plato's Cave. According to Plato, the limited world of appearance in which unemancipated men

20. The above citations are from Édouard Dujardin, *Le Monologue intérieur* (Paris, 1931), pp. 14, 11–12, 42, 48. Cf. this work, *passim*, together with the writers whom he quotes. Cf. also Kurt Jäckel, *Bergson und Proust* (Breslau, 1934).

lead their imprisoned life is a place of darkness surrounded by a region of light. For
Lawrence, on the other hand, the cave is a
place of artificial light surrounded by the reality of darkness. In Plato the emancipation
of true philosophy consists in escaping in-
definiteness through the use of concepts and
dialectic; for Lawrence emancipation consists
in escaping the definiteness of the intellect
through a reliance on instinct and feeling.
Literature, as Lawrence conceives it, teaches
men to move or even to see in the dark,—in
that darkness which pervades the primeval
reality and constitutes its native hue.[21] There
is a hint or at least a parody of James in this.

I would not press these analogies too far,
still less deny that in the artistic experience
and achievement some characteristic and
unique principle of selection is introduced—
so that what is morally, scientifically, or logically irrelevant must be artistically relevant.
But there is a residual correctness in the comparison. In both cases, in modern art and in
the metaphysics of James, there is an effort to
undo selection, and to recover the original
plenum of experience. In both cases, too, there
is a recognition that for conscious experience,

21. Cf. Aldous Huxley, *The Olive Tree and Other Essays* (1937), pp. 210–211.

since consciousness is selective, the data of thought and sense are accompanied by preferential attitudes and fused with these into a concreteness to which the dilemma of subjectivity or objectivity can only inaptly be applied.

A writer of the present day has remarked of most of the issues which concerned James that "if they have not been settled," they have "at least paled a little, displaced by more crying problems."[22] At least one of James's issues, not mentioned by this writer, appears at the moment to have become the central issue of philosophy. It was, I think, the issue which James himself, had he been forced to judge, would have deemed the most fateful. The advance of "instrumentalism" and "operationalism" in the experimental sciences, of symbolism in logic, and of logico-experimental positivism in sociology and philosophy, have created a new cult which touches human thought at all points and threatens a profound and epochal change in the intellectual life of the Western world. It is the fitting philosophical expression of an age of technology. This cult teaches that knowledge, in the maximal or

22. Suzanne K. Langer, "On a Fallacy in 'Scientific Fatalism,'" *International Journal of Ethics*, XLVI, No. 4 (July, 1936), 473.

preferred sense, deals with signs and experimental operations. Definitions in these terms are substituted for the originals. Logicomathematical theories and experimental projects being elaborated and verified, knowledge may thereafter proceed as though there were only signs and operations. I have no desire to dispute the propriety of this view as a description or program of scientific method. Still less do I desire to disparage the achievements of science, weaken its prestige, or compromise the rigor of its procedure. I wish only to insist that there is, unmistakably and undisputably, a variegated panorama of qualities and a warmth of emotional response which formal and quantitative knowledge omits. Their omission is no less an omission for being conscious and methodical. They are not annihilated when they are relegated to poetry. The only effect is to give a new dignity to poetry. And it is at least an open question whether the terms of formal discourse and the constructions of experimental inquiry are not themselves derived from, and referent to, those very qualities and feelings for which they are substituted. In any case, he who by discernment or affection is aware of the field of original meanings knows that for which there is no other equivalent. It is at least a part of the purpose of philosophy to invite men to sense and feel their world. No one has issued this call more eloquently, or himself responded to it more fruitfully and contagiously, than William James.

CHAPTER IV

A MILITANT LIBERAL

THIRTY-FIVE years ago, in an address before the Graduate School of Arts and Sciences at Harvard University, James spoke words which he might have uttered today with even greater force, and with new applications. He said:

Speaking broadly, there are never more than two fundamental parties in a nation: the party of red blood, as it calls itself, and that of pale reflection: the party of animal instinct, jingoism, fun, excitement, bigness; and that of reason, forecast, order gained by growth, and spiritual methods—briefly put, the party of force and that of education. . . . The Tories in any country and the mob will always pull together in the red-blood party, when the catchwords are properly manipulated . . . ; and liberalism will be between the upper and the nether millstone. . . . The chronic fault of liberalism is its lack of speed and passion.[1]

Today there may be doubt as to whether the Tories and the mob will always pull together, but there can be no doubt of the jeopardy of

1. Perry, *op. cit.*, II, 299.

liberalism. Between the upper millstone of fascism and the lower millstone of communistic revolt it has in many countries been ground to extinction, and where it still survives it has lost prestige and dynamic power. Its fault, in an age of acute emergency and of inflamed emotion, is still "its lack of speed and passion."

Assuming the liberal to be right, how can he be effective? How can he mix enough heat with his light, and enough conviction with his honest doubts, to influence the course of human affairs, or even to save himself? How can he be true to his purpose of peace and moderation, and yet be militant enough, defensively and offensively, to prevail, or even survive, in an age when every faction carries arms and marches to warlike music? It so happens that James not only prophesied this hour of crisis, but in his own person and philosophy pointed the way by which it can be met. From him we shall seek to learn how liberalism can be militant, and how militancy can be illuminated by the spirit of liberalism.

James's metaphysics is, as we have seen, a metaphysics of concrete or plenary experience. To know in the most complete sense is to be acquainted with the scene, and to assume over and above its limited region of exposure, depths unplumbed and expanses untraversed, which continue it beyond. Metaphysics is opposed to morals, because metaphysics is a discounting of choice. Man is essentially a choosing animal, but in metaphysics he surmounts his choice through becoming conscious of it. Choice misleads those who, being governed by motives which they are unable or unwilling to admit, confuse their selections with the absolute or aboriginal totality. James's metaphysics is not "humanistic" in this restrictive sense. It reveals material fit for the builder's hands, but is not an artefact, even on the grand cosmic scale. So to consider the universe would be to trivialize it, by identifying it with some form imposed upon it by the interest of the subject. The empirical universe is a *field of options*, together with the acts of choice which arise within this field and the selections and achievements which these acts define. It offers the subject this and that, to which his emotional nature may respond with favor or aversion. It is a world to be liked or disliked, adopted or rejected, supported or opposed. As these acts occur there arise within the world what it is now customary to call "values." In the last analysis the question of value is the question, brought home to some interested subject: "Do I enjoy this sensed quality? Shall I seek to perpetuate it? Shall

I endeavor to bring into existence this pattern of qualities which my imagination constructs from the data of experience?" The ultimate preferences which confer value on their objects are conditioned by the sensible presentation of their objects or by their imaginative reproduction or reconstruction. The given world lends itself to these partisanships and lets them fight it out among themselves. The metaphysician will respect the world for its very neutrality and indifference; or, for its giving itself so promiscuously to all causes as to keep everybody in doubt as to the outcome.

James relished this aspect of chaotic plenitude which experience exhibits when it is restored to its primitive unselectedness. Not only did he take it to be metaphysically revealing, but he enjoyed its contemplation. It suited his taste in universes. Nevertheless despite his aesthetic sensibility, James's fundamental values were practical and moral. The given world *was* there to appreciate contemplatively, but with James its appeal was primarily to the will. It was a potentiality of action—plastic enough to afford a hope of success—but sufficiently resistant and uncertain to impart an element of risk. He was himself one of the partisans. Characterizing Santayana as "a spectator rather than an actor

by temperament," James said in his own behalf that those who "insist that the ideal and
the real are dynamically continuous are those
by whom the world is to be saved." In short,
James's world was a world to be saved, by
changing it into more perfect accord with the
ideal end which his will chose to adopt. Evil,
the inverse of the ideal, was not to be tolerated, or merely viewed with distaste, but remedied or uprooted. "To hate evil does not mean
to indulge in a brooding feeling against particular evils; that is, to be possessed by it. No,
it is to avert the attention, till your chance
comes, and then strike home."[2]

Among the criticisms of James there is none
which seems to me so strangely superficial as
that of Van Wyck Brooks, who accuses James
of a failure to create "values," and of encour-
aging an acquiescence in American standards
of expediency:

By giving a fresh *cachet* to the ordinary work-
ing creed of a pioneer civilization, James led his
disciples back into the wilderness from which
they might otherwise have emerged; and there
he left them. And their impulses trickled away
into the sand. . . . He was unable to create
values because he had never transcended his en-

2. Perry, *op. cit.*, II, 270, 271; *The Letters of William
James* (1920), II, 123; and cf. *idem*, II, 699.

vironment, and his failure to do so is perhaps typical of the failures of all those other men who might have deepened and strengthened the character of our society. . . . James's whole life . . . was thus plainly, in its effort to achieve "healthy-mindedness," an effort also to reconcile himself, to bring himself into rapport with a busy, practical, "tough-minded" world, an effort in which, in order to play the game, he gradually and unconsciously surrendered his belief in the final importance of any values superior to those that were current in the American society of his day.[3]

This writer nowhere tells us precisely what he means by "values," but I gather from the context that he means the adoption of some hierarchy of ends dominated by an ultimate goal of one's own choosing and pursued with heroic resolution. There is, no doubt, some force in the charge that all moralists, James included, exalt the will above the feelings, and emphasize the "humanitarian" *distribution* of goods rather than their "humanistic" or cultural *quality*. But if the critic means that James embodied or taught the vulgar code of success, there could be no more inexcusable misunderstanding. He was usually in the minority, risking his safety in the front ranks

3. *Sketches in Criticism* (1932), pp. 40, 42.

of some unpopular cause. He felt that the
"educated" man was doomed to lose most of
his battles, buoyed only by the devout hope
that he might nevertheless prevail in the long
campaign of light against the brutal forces of
darkness. That which made "life worth living," and which he characteristically detected
in humble as well as in exalted circles, was the
willingness of men to meet nature with spiritual violence, imposing some higher good
upon a hostile, or at best reluctant, environment. *"Character,"* he said, "everywhere demands the stern and sacrificial mood. . . .
The price must be paid."[4] No European or
American moralist has more eloquently ex-
horted every man to fight for the faith that is
in him. Indeed so strong was James's insistence on this cult of moral heroism that the
central difficulty in his ethics is the reconciliation of this cult with his fundamental benevolence.[5]

For James was a heroic and fighting partisan, who gave his final allegiance to the
cause of kindness and peace. This paradox is
so central not only to James, but to the whole
cult of liberalism, that I should like to trans-

4. Perry, *op. cit.,* II, 271.
5. Cf. above, chap. I, pp. 22–23.

late it into my own terms, and formulate it as the conflict between the *exclusive* and the *inclusive* principles of life.

By the exclusive principle I mean that principle which justifies devotion to one's own cause at the expense of others; and by the inclusive principle, that which requires that concessions be made to all individuals concerned, in the interest of their aggregate fulfillment. To understand the full force of this conflict it is necessary to observe that exclusive ends may be of the type commonly regarded as moral. That specific appetites are exclusive in their implications is plain enough. He who follows the dictates of an appetite wherever they may lead will ruthlessly negate such appetites, one's own or others', as happen to be incompatible. But the same is true of such an ideal as self-realization. The ideal of personal self-development or self-fulfillment will, if followed exclusively, bring its adherents into conflict with other adherents of this or of some different end. The same is true of class interests, such as those embodied in aristocracies or dictatorships; and is commonly true of the cult of nationalism. Most qualitative and formal codes have a like exclusiveness. The cult of humanistic culture, if taken to mean the development of the highest human faculties in the most gifted members of the race, implies a disregard of the demands of less qualified men. Even the code of duty for duty's sake may be taken to imply that the agent gives his allegiance to the dictates of his inner conscience, come what may to others. Finally, that very code of heroism which James himself so often commends is, if taken as supreme, likewise exclusive. For heroism is no less heroic if it is realized at the expense of others; indeed the most heroic moments in the history of mankind are those in which man has been at war with man, and in which the hero has been as pitiless as he has been brave.

Over against these exclusive codes there is a principle which has been at work from the beginning of human history, and which has been the most powerful ideal force in the foundation and shaping of human institutions. It is characteristic of human life, in all its spheres and epochs, that interest is in conflict with interest, person with person, class with class, and nation with nation. This all-pervasive and chronic situation begets a specific problem, the problem, namely, of plotting a course of action that shall take account of all the interests at stake. The organization of the personal life endeavors to introduce a reign of peaceful prosperity among the warring appetites and impulses of the same individual; the state and other social institutions endeavor to do the same for the individuals and classes who are members of one group; diplomacy, international law, arbitration, and leagues of nations seek likewise, albeit with small success, to define a policy that shall satisfy all of the interested groups that compose contemporary mankind. This is what I propose to call the principle of inclusiveness.

Let me interpret this principle further in terms of three interdependent ideas, all of which are familiar catchwords of liberalism: individualism, liberty, and tolerance. They can best be understood in terms of a more general idea that applies to all of them, and is the essence of that liberality in which they participate—the idea, namely, of *otherness*. Individualism taken as the mere self-affirmation of an individual is the root of all exclusiveness. In its disregard of others it is what is popularly called "selfishness." *Inclusive* individualism, on the other hand, means that one individual respects other individuals. He acknowledges the same right of self-affirmation in others which he claims for himself; and he rejoices in the numerous individualities and forms of social intercourse which this acknowledgment engenders. A man is a liberal not by virtue of being himself an individual, but by virtue of acknowledging and enjoying other individuals.

Similarly, the love of one's own liberty is implied in every moving interest, meaning only that each pursues its goal with passionate insistence, and with resentment felt toward any force which blocks the path or any competing interest which appropriates the desired object. The dog who snarls at an intruder who would deprive him of his bone is the perfect embodiment of this love of one's *own* liberty. I would not belittle the importance of this will to be let alone and to do as one pleases. It is a characteristic of all free societies and a condition of resolute achievement. But a man is not liberal in spirit, or in his heart a devotee of what I have called inclusiveness, until he justly concedes and ardently desires the liberty of another.

The same is true, and peculiarly true, of tolerance. The question of tolerance arises from the fact that other individuals are other not merely in a numerical sense, but in a qualitative sense as well. They are not only other but *different*. Other individuals possess the general human characteristics, giving to these multiple and competitive embodiment. But they also possess idiosyncrasies contrast-

ing with one's own. Now the wish to enjoy
and manifest one's own idiosyncrasies without
interference is the disposition of every man,
and earns no moral credit. Tolerance, in the
deeper and moral sense, is the disposition to
enjoy, or at least to suffer patiently, the idiosyncrasies of *others*, precisely in those respects in which they are dissimilar to one's
own.

It is the same with the tolerance of belief.
If one has beliefs at all one wants them to be
tolerated, which means only that one wants to
be allowed to believe one's beliefs—to profess
them and to propagate them. The greater a
man's conviction of the truth of his beliefs the
greater his resentment of any agency or authority which seeks to suppress them. Those
who resist persecution, or fly to escape it, are
not on that account exponents of tolerance.
They may be, and are likely to be, the most
uncompromising and dogmatic partisans.
They ask to *be tolerated*, but they are not tolerant. When such fierce sectarians abound it
becomes the part of statesmanship, in the interest of public peace, to define and guarantee
certain liberties of thought, speech and assembly for all. Sectarianism forces the issue
of tolerance, and leads to the creation of liberal institutions. But the first tolerant man

is not he who merely demands tolerance and
enjoys its application to himself, but he who
values it as a social good. Thus the conflict of
beliefs may suggest to a critical observer that
the cool examination of evidence is a more
promising road to truth than passionate adherence to a creed; that truth is many sided,
and that the whole truth is a reconciliation
and summation of the many truths attained
by the severalty of individuals, each faithful
to his own insight; or that the final truth in
the matters concerned is so doubtful as to dis-
credit every hard and exclusive opinion. From
this reflective attitude may spring a positive
desire that opinion—the other's opinion as
well as one's own—shall be delivered from the
coercion of authority. One may become the advocate of free discussion, believing in its fecundity; or of the right of every other to his
own faith, where certain knowledge is impossible. The degree of a man's tolerance in the
inclusive sense will be measured by his willingness that other opinions, even contrary opinions, which he holds to be false or improbable,
should nevertheless be allowed expression; and
by his willingness to concede this liberty of
expression in matters that he holds to be of
profound importance—in religious matters,
when these seem most urgent, in political and

economic matters when these in turn are the
burning issues of the day. For otherwise he is
at best indifferent, rather than tolerant.

In the light of these general considerations
let me turn again to James. The idea of otherness pervaded his entire philosophy. In his
metaphysics of experience he stressed the variety of existence, and the need of a generous
acknowledgment of strangeness and novelty
as the first attribute of the philosophic mind.
So characteristic was this quality of intellectual magnanimity that it is permissible to
say that his moral liberalism was but an application of his basic principles. Referring to
his "pluralistic or individualistic philosophy,"
he said:

According to that philosophy, the truth is too
great for any one actual mind . . . to know the
whole of it. The facts and worths of life need
many cognizers to take them in. . . . The practical consequence of such a philosophy is the
well-known democratic respect for the sacredness of individuality.[6]

It will be noted that the moral quality he
praises is not the individuality itself, but *the
feeling of its sacredness.*

6. *Talks to Teachers* (1899), Preface, p. v.

The essay on "The Moral Philosopher and the Moral Life" (1891)[7] is James's only sustained discussion of ethical first principles. The ethics of inclusiveness which is there formulated grew out of his lectures in Philosophy 4, given in 1888–89. The following extracts are taken from his notes for that course:

Man spontaneously *believes* and spontaneously *acts*. But as acts and beliefs multiply they grow inconsistent. To escape *bellum omnium contra omnes*, reasonable principles, fit for all to agree upon, must be sought. . . . The abstract best would be that *all* goods should be realized. That is physically impossible, for many of them exclude each other. . . . But how decide conflicts? . . . Sacrifice all wills which are not organizable, and which avowedly go against the whole. . . . When the rivalry is between real organizable goods, the rule is that the one victorious should so far as possible keep the vanquished somehow represented. Find some innocent way out.[8]

For James the fundamental purpose is to seek, as he puts it, "principles fit for all to agree upon"; to find "some innocent way out," that is, some way that offends no interest,

7. Reprinted in *The Will to Believe* (1897), pp. 184–215.
8. Perry, *op. cit.*, II, 263, 264, 265.

every interest having been consulted in advance and converted to its support. Such a solution is not always possible. Its impossibility represents, as judged by the principle of inclusiveness, a moral failure. The principle itself is a norm, an ideal end to be pursued, and, so far as the conditions of life permit, approximated.

When James dealt explicitly with political and social problems, he used this norm. When he participated actively in public affairs it was to reveal this purpose. He became the advocate of some neglected individual, some small nation, some despised cause, some humble sphere of life whose sacred inwardness had escaped the gross or insolent judgment of the world. He championed their claim to be reckoned in the sum of goods or in the sum of wisdom, and their right to be included in any plan of public life. He was himself one of those "generous characters" of whom he said, with no suspicion of self-praise, that they "sympathize with the free flow of things"; and who

when they profess . . . that certain persons should be free . . . mean it not as most of us do—with a mental reservation, as that the freedom should be well employed and other similar humbug—but in all sincerity, and calling for no guarantee against abuse which, when it happens, they accept without complaint or embitterment as part of the chances of the game. They let their bird fly with no string tied to its leg.

Peculiarly characteristic of James, in fact the quintessential flavor of his liberalism, was his extension of hospitality beyond the limits of understanding. He was willing, nay delighted, to suffer the existence of "many another queer and wondrous and only half-delightful thing." The "sight of elephants and tigers at Barnum's," evoked in James a willingness to embrace within his world lives with which one could not pretend to sympathize, but which were nevertheless so admirable in their own terms that one yearned to be their "sharer, partner or accomplice." "Their foreignness," he said, "confounds one's pretension to comprehend the world,—while their admirableness undermines the stoic . . . frame of mind in which one says the real meaning of life is *my* action."[9]

Twenty-five years later James described the true spirit of liberalism as a glad willingness that other beings, however different and incommensurable their value, should live their own lives in their own way. Such a spirit

9. Perry, *op. cit.*, II, 269, 268.

is negative in one sense, but positive in another. It absolutely forbids us to be forward in pronouncing on the meaninglessness of forms of existence other than our own; and it commands us to tolerate, respect, and indulge those whom we see harmlessly interested and happy in their own ways, however unintelligible these may be to us. Hands off: neither the whole of truth nor the whole of good is revealed to any single observer, although each observer gains a partial superiority of insight from the peculiar position in which he stands. Even prisons and sick-rooms have their special revelations. It is enough to ask of each of us that he should be faithful to his own opportunities and make the most of his own blessings, without presuming to regulate the rest of the vast field.[10]

This means that the liberal will possess an indeterminate or blanket tolerance—a consent—a desire, that others should think for themselves, *whatever they think,* or should pursue their own ends, *whatever ends they be.* It implies an acceptance in advance of the consequences of liberty, however novel and unpredictable, and however great the shock to one's personal prepossessions. It means not that otherness should be reluctantly conceded, or bravely endured, but welcomed with a glad heart. It means that one should rejoice in the

10. *Talks to Teachers,* etc. (1899), pp. 263–64.

surprising and the unintelligible. The evidence of liberty in others is their departure from my accustomed ways, their breach of my rules, their opaqueness to my vision, their inexplicableness by my theories, their irrelevance to my purposes; and I cannot be said to be a lover of liberty unless I love its evidences, or until these very contrarieties to my own subjective bias are zestfully acclaimed.

James was the exponent of a fighting faith, and an admirer of those heroic qualities which mark the devotee of a cause: he chose his cause and adhered to it exclusively. But the cause which he chose was the cause of inclusiveness: he was an advocate of individualism, of liberty, and of tolerance, which seems to imply a sympathetic, or at least magnanimous, attitude to *all* faiths and causes. How are these strains of exclusiveness and inclusiveness to be reconciled? Before I set forth what I believe to be James's solution, or the solution most consistent with his teachings, let us examine a plausible alternative.

In his admirable lectures on *The Great Chain of Being,* Professor Lovejoy has recently discussed what he calls the "diversitarianism" of the romantic movement, or the cult of "differentness":

It came to be believed not only that in many, or in all, phases of human life there are diverse excellences, but that diversity itself is of the essence of excellence; and that of art, in particular, the objective is . . . the fullest possible expression of the abundance of differentness that there is, actually or potentially, in nature and human nature. . . . [This is] the one *common* . . . factor in a number of otherwise diverse tendencies which, by one or another critic or historian, have been termed "Romantic": the immense multiplication of genres and verseforms; the admission of the aesthetic legitimacy of the *genre mixte;* the *goût de la nuance;* the naturalization in art of the "grotesque"; the quest for local color; the endeavor to reconstruct in imagination the distinctive inner life of peoples remote in time or space or in cultural condition; the *étalage du moi;* the demand for particularized fidelity in landscape-description; the revulsion against simplicity; the distrust of universal formulas in politics; the aesthetic antipathy to standardization; the identification of the Absolute with the "concrete universal" in metaphysics; the feeling of "the glory of the imperfect"; the cultivation of individual, national, and racial peculiarities; the depreciation of the obvious and the general high valuation (wholly foreign to most earlier periods) of originality, and the usually futile and absurd self-conscious pursuit of that attribute.

As the author has pointed out, this cult encourages that very power of imaginative sympathy which James has praised and which he himself so notably possessed:

On the one hand, it suggested, as both an aesthetic and a moral aim for the individual, the effort to enter as fully as possible into the immensely various range of thought and feeling in other men. It thus made for the cultivation, not merely of tolerance, but of imaginative insight into the points of view, the valuations, the tastes, the subjective experiences, of others; and this not only as a means to the enrichment of one's own inner life, but also as a recognition of the objective validity of diversities of valuation. The Romantic imperative, so construed, was: "Respect and delight in—not merely, as with Kant, the universal reason in which all men uniformly participate—but the qualities by which men, and all creatures, are unlike one another and, in particular, are unlike yourself." "I almost believe"—wrote Friedrich Schlegel— "that a wise self-limitation and moderation of the mind is not more necessary to man than the inward, ever restless, almost voracious, participation in all life, and a certain feeling of the sanctity (*Heiligkeit*) of an abounding fullness."[11]

11. Arthur O. Lovejoy, *The Great Chain of Being* (1936), pp. 293–294, 304–305; cf. p. 313.

Notwithstanding the similarity between James and romanticism, the former as an empiricist belongs to a fundamentally different philosophical school. Romanticism is a phase in the development of absolutism. Beneath its emphasis on multiplicity and difference there lies the affirmation of a metaphysical unity. The romanticist may seek to reconcile this unity with the facts of diversity in one of two ways. He may find the unity in the very fullness of diversity itself—taken as a maximum of qualitative possibility, or as a dramatization of contrast and tension. In this case the fact that the differences are conflicting in no way detracts from the unity which they compose. Or he may find the unity in a resolution of conflict imputed to some metaphysical reality beyond the plane of human experience. Harmony is affirmed *a priori* or taken on faith. In either case each constituent element of life is justified in asserting itself unqualifiedly—conscious of its unique contribution to the variegated whole, or confident that a higher being will provide the resolution. Thus romanticism lends itself readily to a ruthless subjectivism or nationalism. It fills the world with prophetic claims which, since they are conflicting, lead to war, and which, since they invoke the same absolute sanction, make war itself fanatical and uncompromising. With James, on the other hand, diversity is a fact, and conflict a regrettable fact: neither is metaphysically necessary. The honest-minded and sensitive observer of life will acknowledge these facts. He will transcend his own subjectivity and give the other, with all its strangeness and contrariety, full credit. This recognition of diverse and antagonistic otherness will stimulate his will, as presenting him with a suitable occasion for action. But it constitutes his realism rather than his idealism,—the material and not the form of his moral will—the problem and not the solution of the moral achievement. The moral achievement itself lies in the reconciliation of diverse claims, or in the achievement of a diversity that shall be innocent and harmonious.

I admit that we must tread our way carefully, and I would not claim that James has uttered no word that might be cited in favor of the romantic interpretation. It is true that James enjoyed his diverse and incoherent world—that it gave him an immediate satisfaction comparable to his preference of the natural wilderness to the Italian garden. It is true that James attached intrinsic value to heroic action, and praised the life of conflict and struggle for the personal qualities which

it engendered. But taking James as a whole
there can, I think, be no shred of doubt that
he regarded these qualities as subordinate in
the moral hierarchy, compensations—yes—
but not to be confused with the consummate
value of peace.

The essential point can be argued in terms
of the antithesis between aestheticism and
moralism. Aestheticism would justify the costs
of conflict by the delectation which the spec-
tacle affords to the observer, or by the exhila-
rating sense of active participation. These
subjective values being supreme, they would
justify the pain inflicted on the victims and
the wickedness which incites righteous indignation. A devotee of aestheticism would even
contemplate with equanimity a world in which
pain and wickedness were, like the painter's
shadows or the playwright's villain, deliberately *contrived* for the aesthetic satisfaction
they afford. The moral will would then be superseded by the aesthetic will, and moral evil
would have become aesthetic good. The moral
will would have been overruled and annulled.
The moral struggle would have become a
sham battle—only the simple-minded would
engage in it without mental reservations. The
emancipated and philosophic mind would enjoy a sense of cynical superiority to both par-

ties, seeing that they were merely the naïve
instruments of destiny, contributing by their
pathetic earnestness to a dramatic effect
which they were themselves too unsophisti-
cated to understand. Were they to become
aware of their roles their hands would be
stayed. They, too, having joined the specta-
tors, the stage would be empty; or if, being
conscious of their roles, they should continue
to perform them, they would do so without
conviction, like actors in a play.

James not only saw this flat contradiction
between the aesthetic and the moral attitudes,
but awarded the second priority over the first,
and gave it his deeper allegiance. The essence
of the matter is that "something is doing in
the universe." "It feels like a real fight" to
which the only suitable response is the "gospel
of work, of fact, or veracity."[12] Thus it comes
in the end to James's empirical realism. Evil
cannot be explained away. Its stark odious-
ness is not to be relieved by any speculative
sleight of hand. The conflict between good
and evil is irreconcilable—that is the undeniable and unpalatable fact; and philosophy is
the brave and candid recognition of the fact.
The recognition of this fact is morally exhila-

12. Perry, *op. cit.*, II, 656; James, "The Sentiment of
Rationality," *The Will to Believe* (1897), p. 87.

rating. But to conceive the exhilaration of the combat as the intrinsic good of which the enemy is therefore the necessary and desirable condition is obfuscation and treason.

There is a kind of reflective moralism, or moralism of second intent, which is as contrary to the meaning of liberalism as is the transformation of moral into aesthetic values. The cult of "rugged individualism" is a case in point. Ruggedness, I take it, refers to the harsher aspects of the struggle for existence, —the emphasis which it places on a capacity both to endure and to inflict hardships. It is one thing to find this capacity admirable when it arises from the given circumstances of life, and is a necessary condition of the effort to improve them. It becomes another and a very different thing at the moment when these circumstances are approved for the sake of the capacities which they require. For at that moment the circumstances, however painful or cruel they may be, are no longer an evil to be overcome, but a good to be acknowledged or perpetuated. And when this shift occurs liberalism is killed at the root. There is no longer any incentive to develop and exercise those very capacities which are admired. The exponent of rugged individualism has become in his heart, if not in his profession or overt action, one who would for the sake of the struggle itself preserve the very poverty, pain, and frustration which he has hitherto struggled to eradicate.

Granted that evil is an undeniable and irreducible fact, the way of righteousness for James is to attack it or "make the best" of it —to overcome and undo it, or, failing this, to bear it without morbid obsession. Incidental to loyal and uncompromising hostility there are values that may even be said to be "intrinsic." Thus courage is in itself good, both admirable to the onlooker and exalting to the moral participant. But their *moral* quality lies in their effects—in their diminution of pain or frustration for all concerned, or in the defeat of counter-forces by which pain and frustration are created. And even the intrinsic values of the martial spirit, both as admired and as enjoyed, presuppose the "reality" of the emergency. For if the evil combated is only a pretext for the exhibition or relish of the martial spirit, this spirit at once becomes trivial; a "mock heroics" or "play acting," when the agent is himself one of the initiated; and a pathetic self-deception when he is not.

Santayana has described James in terms that aptly express the spirit of liberalism. "Nobody," he writes, "ever recognised more heartily the chance that others had of being right, and the right they had to be different." But the essay in which this characterization appears is at the same time a criticism of James and of liberals in general, on the ground that they had no conception of the good life. "They had," he said, "forgotten the Greeks." But Santayana, though he was and is a distinguished moral diagnostician, and has with rare poetic sensitiveness elucidated a realm of essences, has somehow failed to intuit the essence of liberalism. How far this essence does or does not coincide with the moral ideal of the Greeks I shall not presume to judge. If that ideal is to be identified with aestheticism and intellectualism, either or both, then James certainly did not forget it, but deliberately rejected it. If, on the other hand, the Greek ideal was heroic manliness, then James's liberalism is neither a forgetting nor a rejection, but a modification. This modification embraces two steps, both of which are no doubt caused or confirmed by the influence of Christianity. In the first place, the emphasis is shifted from physical to moral heroism; in the second place, moral heroism is purged of selfishness or partisan exclusiveness, and rendered all-inclusively humane. Waiving the question of its rank in the hierarchy of value, the ideal which results is as much an essence, or form of admirable and enjoyable goodness, as any poetic vision of ancient Greece, whether manly virtue, graciousness, or the theoretic exercise of reason. To open one's eyes to the facts of human misery and frustration, to feel their massive proportions by the extension of sympathy, to sense the pathos of the aggregate life, to carry in one's heart a heavy burden of solicitude, to feel an eagerness to help and remedy and save, to live generously and lovingly—these elements compose a form of excellence as intrinsically admirable and profoundly enjoyable as any aspect of paganism, whether remembered or forgotten. And the organized benevolence which is the active expression of this ideal strains the resources of every human faculty. "Liberty," says Santayana, "is not an art."[13] Never was a falser statement more wittily made. If liberty means only the self-assertion of an appetite, it is not an art, but only the forward thrust which belongs aboriginally to every interest. But if liberty means the conceding of liberty, the delimitation and distribution of liberties within a social order, then it is perhaps the most dif-

13. *Character and Opinion in the United States* (1920), pp. 93, 85–86, 91.

ficult, as it is the most urgent and fruitful, of
all arts.

We are now in a position to attack the central problem of this chapter, the reconciliation, namely, of a provident and tolerant
humanitarianism with the militant will—of
the ideal of inclusiveness with the temper of
exclusiveness. How is it possible to take sides,
as the moral will must, and wage war upon
the opposing side, as such a will implies; and
at the same time with humane sympathy and
understanding credit the opponent with a like
right to *his* cause, and with magnanimous detachment approve the very zest which ani-
mates the opponent's defense and counterat-
tack? How is a belief "in the reign of peace
and in the gradual advent of some sort of a
socialistic equilibrium"[14] to be reconciled with
that "marriage of some unhabitual ideal, however special, with some fidelity, courage, and
endurance" which always constitutes "the
solid meaning of life"?

That it is humanly possible to associate the
creed of liberalism with the spirit of militancy
James has proved both by precept and example. Apropos of the prediction by pessi-

14. James, *Memories and Studies* (1912), p. 286.

mistic critics that democracy would end as "vulgarity enthroned and institutionalized," James said:

No one with a spark of reason in him will sit down fatalistically before the croaker's picture. The best of us are filled with the contrary vision of a democracy stumbling through every error till its institutions glow with justice and its customs shine with beauty.[15]

The liberal will with all his might oppose the exploitation of official power, the greed of imperialism, the cruelty of racial prejudice, and the ruthlessness of war.[16] He will cultivate the martial traits. But for the school of physical warfare on which the race has hitherto depended for the cultivation of "intrepidity, contempt of softness, surrender of private interest, obedience to command,"[17] James would substitute the school of productive labor, enlisting men to fight against the forces of nature rather than against one another. Life may still be dramatized and the forces of righteousness may still feel the solidarity and élan of combat:

The great international and cosmopolitan lib-

15. *Idem,* pp. 316, 317–318.
16. Cf. Perry, *op. cit.,* II, 290.
17. James, *Memories and Studies* (1912), pp. 287–288.

eral party, the party of conscience and intelligence the world over, has, in short, absorbed us; and we are only its American section, carrying on the war against the powers of darkness here, playing our part in the long, long campaign for truth and fair dealing which must go on in all the countries of the world until the end of time. Let us cheerfully settle into our interminable task. Everywhere it is the same struggle under various names,—light against darkness, right against might, love against hate. The Lord of life is with us, and we cannot permanently fail.[18]

But while it is psychologically possible thus to associate liberalism with militancy, is it morally or logically possible? Does not the belligerent liberal betray his own principles? Does he not when waging war in the name of liberalism contradict his own creed, and cease to be liberal?

It is clear that this question cannot be answered unless the relevant principles of political liberalism are explicitly stated. For present purposes there are two. In the first place, liberalism seeks to promote and safeguard the maximum of liberty that is consistent with public peace. In the second place, liberalism bases public authority on agree-

18. "Address by Prof. William James," *Report of the Fifth Annual Meeting of the New England Anti-Imperialist League, Nov. 28, 1903,* p. 26.

ment, that is, on the thoughtful and deliberate consent of all parties. There will, therefore, be two reasons why a liberal society will tolerate diversity of opinion: because the liberty to think for oneself is one of those liberties which men prize, and which they are entitled to enjoy to any degree short of violence and mutual destruction; and because unless men are allowed to think for themselves it is impossible to win their thoughtful and deliberate assent.

Within the framework of a liberal society dedicated to the principle of inclusiveness, our problem presents no fundamental difficulty. A liberal polity is designed to harbor differences of opinion, and to reconcile these differences with public order. The broad principles of liberalism are so broad that they leave open innumerable special issues of public policy, and as regards these questions liberalism itself is neutral. Those who oppose one another on these special issues are still partners in liberalism, and stand in agreement on that creed which underlies the state itself. No degree of militancy among such partisans is to be considered illiberal, provided it restricts itself to criticism, discussion, and persuasion. Such a partisan is in deed as well as profession an exponent of liberalism, and his very partisanship for his own ideas illustrates its meaning. The liberal in power will respect the liberty of individuals and groups to form opposing opinions, and to agitate and organize in their behalf. Dissenting minorities, being thus protected, will bide their time, seeking by criticism to unseat the party in power and thus eventually to use the instrumentalities of government for the execution of their own policies.

There is, however, a deeper question, and from this there springs a grave and sobering difficulty. What conduct does liberalism dictate toward a party which is professedly and explicitly illiberal? Today it is clear, as never before, that the liberal is confronted with a declared enemy other than physical nature or any impersonal obstacle, a human enemy which openly professes darkness, force, and hate. There is a party of exclusiveness, in which all the stubborn selfishnesses are allied, —the party of war which fights the last fight against the party of peace. How shall a liberal, professing tolerance and peace, not be intolerant of his avowedly intolerant opponent, or the pacifist avoid the use of physical weapons against the enemy in arms?

This question assumes different forms, according as the liberal is in power or out of

power. Suppose a state, pledged to liberal
principles, and confronted with an opposition
pledged to the destruction of those principles.
Shall such a liberal state use illiberal methods
to prevent the incubation and ascent to power
of an illiberal regime? Shall liberals tolerate
the growth of a party whose adherents are resolved to use the agencies of the state to destroy tolerance? Suppose, for example, that
a German liberal of today reflects that Hitler
came into power by a popular election. Let us
assume that this election was "free," or free
enough to constitute a rough approximation
to the opinion and sentiment of the majority.
Having come into power, Hitler has used that
power to outlaw opposition and rob the liberal of his weapons of peaceful persuasion.
Such a helpless and hopeless liberal is likely
to say that in 1933 he was "weak," since he
permitted his opponents by their constitutional victory to render such constitutional
procedure forever impossible in the future.
Using the instruments of press, public speech,
party organization, and free elections to gain
office, these opponents have used that office, or
misused it, so as to prevent such instruments
from ever being used again. Reflecting upon
this outcome, and resenting their plight, it is
not surprising that such liberals should regret

that they did not strangle the monster in its cradle. In their present predicament they have no alternative but *impotent* violence— then, violence might have been effective. If this argument were valid, then it would teach a lesson for the future. It would imply that liberals should resort to force against all cults which profit by liberality in their beginnings in order to destroy it, root and branch, when they are in control.

This mode of reasoning has a wide application. It argues that the tolerant should exterminate the intolerant in infancy, that pacifists should exterminate militarists, that democrats should exterminate authoritarians, that Protestants should exterminate Catholics. Attack first, while you have the chance, lest later you be condemned to a hopeless resistance, in which your conduct will be equally repugnant to your principles but without the compensatory advantage of success!

This conclusion, plausible as it is, cannot be reconciled with the liberal's two basic political principles—of maximum liberty, and of control by agreement. These principles forbid that a liberal state, which is to remain liberal, should suppress any cult, any cult whatsoever, including the cult of illiberalism itself, so long as its adherents observe that fundamental law by which a liberal state reconciles the liberty of one individual or group with the enjoyment of a like liberty by others, and thus reconciles diversity of opinion with public order. The liberty of rejecting the liberal ideology is a form of the right to think for oneself, and this right, like all rights, is limited only by its mutuality. If a man desires to think and his thinking leads him to the rejection of such ideas as tolerance and popular government, then he has a right so to think, provided this does not then and there interfere with others' thinking differently. If the opponents of a liberal regime are to be won to its thoughtful and deliberate support, then their minds must be free. A support won in any other way, as by intimidation or emotional propaganda, is not that rational assent from which a liberal regime professes to derive its authority. If a liberal regime is not willing to submit its case to argument, then its proponents do not believe in its truth, but are merely its fanatical partisans.

An oppressive liberalism borrows not only the practice, but the doctrine of the opponent. It would be based on the same distrust of discussion and of the saving power of truth that underlies all illiberal philosophies. It would not only convert liberality into illiberality,

but precipitate that which it most abhors. It
would take the initiative in substituting force
for reason. It would justify the opponent and
belie every argument that has been brought
against him, as revolution justifies counterrevolution. It would bring about that condition of society in which liberalism is least
likely to gain a hearing—an atmosphere of
violence, a destruction of moral checks and
habits, an intensification of fear and suspicion. It would debase the liberal to the level of
his adversary. For the adversary, too, has his
hopes of the future, and will always tell you
that when his violence has been successful, and
society purged or transformed, then violence
will be no longer necessary and men will be
left to the free exercise of their better reason.

What alternatives remain? The answer is
not easy. There is no simple formula by which
tragic mistakes and subsequent regrets can
be avoided. This much is clear. The liberal in
power, or acting as a partisan under constitutional guarantees, is entitled to every form of
persuasive militancy, such as organization
and propaganda, that the laws allows. If he
is wise he will not in the future underestimate
his enemies or assume that any liberal regime
once inaugurated will survive on its merits.
He will be as vigilant and aggressive as his

opponents. He will ally himself with all parties which are enlisted in the same general cause. He will utilize the agency of the law to suppress all resort to violence, and to prevent such quasi-military organization and distribution of arms and munitions among political factions as encourage the resort to force and excite the fears which lead to countermeasures of the same type. Above all he will keep the edge of his conscience sharp and his righteous indignation warm. Though he abstain from violence, his hostility will be not less relentless. His restraint is not a compromise of ends but only a choice of means. Conscious and methodical illiberality is and remains his deadly foe with which he is engaged in a war of extermination. He will lose no chance of declaring his opinion. Aldous Huxley has said that "one of the principal functions of a friend is to suffer (in a milder and symbolic form) the punishment that we should like, but are unable, to inflict upon our enemies."[19] The liberal, restrained from violence, will fill the air about him with the voice of his hostility, and his friends, as well as the enemy, must if needs be suffer. He will not subordinate his conscience to any considerations of good taste or easy amiability. He will make a nuisance of

19. *Brave New World* (1932), p. 214.

himself both to the enemy and to indifferent
bystanders. If he is unhappily defeated and if
his enemies in power destroy the political instruments of liberalism, then, being denied any
other course, he will take what desperate measures he can. He will endeavor to endure
against the day when a successful revolution
is possible.

The legitimate use of force to suppress dissent begins where dissent employs force. A
liberal regime is under the same obligation to
prohibit lawlessness as any other regime. The
fact that its fundamental law is liberal, and
therefore as indulgent as possible to liberty,
does not diminish this obligation. When,
therefore, the adherent of illiberalism acts in
accordance with his ideas and thus violates
the liberal law under which he lives, it is not
only legal, but on liberal premises, right and
reasonable that he should be deterred by the
fear of penalties. Whether his act is or is not
a violation of law is for the courts, and in the
last analysis for courts having competence in
constitutional law, to decide. Such courts, if
they are parts of a liberal regime, are bound
in their decisions by the principles of liberalism. The illegal and therefore rightly punish-
able in a liberal state is what its courts decide,
and if their decisions are illiberal, then, on

liberal premises, the fault lies there, and is to be remedied by liberalizing the courts, rather than by defying them.

The precise point at which a liberal regime should suppress opposition will turn on the temper and circumstance of concrete situations. All questions of liberty of assembly, of speech and press, involve a line which is difficult to draw between the advocacy of revolutionary ideas and incitement to revolutionary action. In a liberal state *all* questions, including liberalism itself, are "open" questions. There is no prevailing system of ideas or persons, even a Constitution or Supreme Court, which can be considered "sacred." There *is* no such thing as sacredness in a liberal society, if by sacredness is meant immunity from criticism. On the other hand, there is no opposition to the prevailing system that *may* not be translated into overt lawlessness. As Judge Learned Hand has expressed it, "words are not only the keys of persuasion, but the triggers of action." Hence the profound, difficult, crucial, and unavoidable question of reconciling the liberties of thought, speech, press, and assembly with public order. Those who are puzzled by this question will do well to read or re-read Professor Zechariah Chafee's book on *Freedom of Speech*. They will there find a

wealth of citation from judicial opinion and
criminal law to show that the interest of liberty can be reconciled with the interest of
stability, order, and unified authority only by
determining in the particular case the point
at which opposition becomes a "proximate
causation" of violence.

To find the line between such incipient violence and the method of persuasion belongs to
the delicate art of liberty. Freedom of opinion
is most in need of protection when the opinion
is unpopular and feeling inflamed. Unpopular
opinions are those that most need protection;
inflamed feeling is that which is most in
need of enlightenment. To quote Sir James
Fitzjames Stephen: "There may indeed be
breaches of the peace which may destroy or
endanger life, limb, or property, and there
may be incitements to such offenses, but no
imaginable censure of the government, *short
of a censure which has an immediate tendency
to produce such a breach of the peace,* ought
to be regarded as criminal." Professor Chafee
sums the matter up in these words: "Thus our
problem of locating the boundary line of free
speech is solved. It is fixed close to the point
where words will give rise to unlawful acts."[20]

20. Zechariah Chafee, Jr., *Freedom of Speech* (1920),
pp. 49, 24, 38; cf. also pp. 53ff.

Although the same criteria apply, let us
consider the other predicament of the liberal
—the case in which the illiberal is in power,
and the liberal in opposition. Suppose the liberal regime to have been overthrown and superseded by a dictatorship which so employs
the means of publicity or the machinery of
election that any liberal opposition which
thereafter limits itself to these weapons seems
foredoomed to failure. Or suppose that the
state, though it professes to act for the public good and to be responsive to the interests
and opinions of all the people, is partial to
special interests, such, for example, as the interest of "big business." Suppose that a capi-
talistic system entrenched in power possesses
so much control over the lives and fortunes of
the mass of mankind, that dissenters fear to
oppose it unless their opposition will be so
deadly and so instantly effective as to insure
them against reprisal. Strike quickly and
strike hard enough to incapacitate your opponent, otherwise you merely antagonize him
and place yourself at his mercy! These are
not absurd suppositions. Many men make
them, and they constitute the logic of economic revolution.

What conduct will liberalism dictate when
it is the creed of an oppressed minority? How

will such a minority, in keeping with its liberalism, endeavor to relieve its condition, and create or restore a liberal regime? The resort to force is here, as in the former case, a last resort. The oppressed liberal will exhaust every possibility of legal change and redress. A resort to force would borrow the weapons and, for the time being, even the creed of the opponent. To precipitate a state of civil war would entail not only losses of life and property, but moral and intellectual losses as well. The horrors of civil war penetrate deep into the soul of man, altering his attitudes and sensibilities. It precipitates an alternation of reprisals. It justifies, and commonly provokes, a counterrevolution. It engenders the habit and tradition of revolution, together with the pervasive fears and suspicions with which this habit is associated. A revolution, even if successful, may well destroy those human feelings and that faith in reason on which liberalism depends, and so indefinitely postpone its establishment.

There is a point of despair at which revolution is justified, just as there is a point of violence at which suppression is justified. The liberal will postpone them both to the remotest possible limit. There is no formula by which these points can be determined. They will depend on circumstances and can never be ascertained with precision. In both cases they signify the utter futility of the method of persuasion, and the liberal will be distinguished by his resort to the method of persuasion even when all others have forsaken it. However militant his faith and zeal for the cause he serves, he will with the utmost reluctance arm himself with physical weapons and abandon the appeal to reason for the appeal to fear.

I HAVE attempted in this chapter to present liberalism, symbolized by William James, as a fighting faith, and to show how its militancy can be reconciled with its creed. Liberalism is a good cause to fight for—its utopian dreams are on the grand scale, and they can be pursued with a good conscience, a whole heart, and the minimum of bitterness. But liberalism is a good creed even for those who by temperament, disability, or failure are excluded from the field of battle. It is a sweeter thing than cynical spectatorship or sore despair—a better mood to live with even in solitude or withdrawal. It enables the consciousness of human limitation to be attended by a patient trust in mankind. Even the sense of futility may be saved from the degradation of contempt, and transmuted into a more ennobling pathos.

The clash and mutual annulment of social causes, the littleness of their victories and the magnitude of their defeats, humanity's blundering confusion and mouselike subjection to the playful brutalities of nature—all this can at least be seen with the eye of loving pity and thus be made to yield some saving sense of tragic exaltation.

CHAPTER V

THE RIGHT TO BELIEVE

THE heading of the present chapter is
one of the alternative titles which James
afterwards wished he had chosen for the famous essay that appeared as "The Will to Believe." The actual title suggested that the
author commended dogmatic and wishful
thinking, whereas his aim was to criticize belief in order to determine the precise conditions under which a scrupulous man may give
his credence to beliefs for which the evidence
is imperfect.[1]

It is sometimes supposed that the recognition of a domain of faith, where belief exceeds
evidence, is characteristic of rationalistic
rather than of empiricist philosophers. The
reverse of this is in fact the case. The ration-
alist credits the pure intellect with a capacity
to prove existence, employing a formula such
as Bradley's "what must be, is." He is not
hampered by the limitations of human experience. The ontological proof, by which the existence of God is deduced from the concept, is
in all its diverse forms, ancient and modern,

1. Cf. Perry, *op. cit.*, II, 243–248.

the work of rationalists. The ideal of scholas-
ticism, according to which the truths of faith
coincide with the truths of reason would, if
realized, have eliminated faith altogether except as an evidence for lesser minds darkened
by sin or arrested in their development. It was
Kant, as opposed to his rationalistic predecessors, who introduced faith on purely philosophical grounds, and he did so because of his
rigorous adherence to the maxim that existence is undemonstrable by reason and must,
if known at all, be given in experience. Hume
affords an equally notable example of a philosopher who, having limited theoretical
knowledge to the verification of actual experience, finds that practical belief must exceed
these bounds. He acknowledged, in short, a
"must believe" which is non-theoretical. And
it is through this door, often casually and in-
conspicuously placed in some obscure part of
the edifice, that most of the traffic passes.
There is, indeed, a curious paradox by which
those philosophers who are most strict and
narrow in their conception of knowledge are
compelled to make the largest provision for
faith. The sceptic must substitute faith for
knowledge altogether. The positivist defines
an area of strict logico-experimental knowledge, but spends most of his cognitive life out

of bounds. More liberal empiricists, like
James, broaden the area of knowledge and
rely less on faith, but still fall far short of
those rationalists who claim to "prove all
things."

Usually faith is a philosophical makeshift,
an emergency entrance, hastily added when
the regular door proves too narrow. With
James, however, the door of faith is placed in
the front elevation. Its ultimate use is reckoned in advance and it forms a part of the
architect's design. James was from the beginning aware that belief serves two masters,
theory and life. We are justified in believing
what is proved, but we are also justified in believing what it is *desirable* or *right to believe.*
These two justifications do not always coincide, there being an excess sometimes on one
side, sometimes on the other. The case in
which there is excess of practical over theoretical justification is the case of "the right to
believe." This is an entirely different doctrine
from that which discovers a practical procedure and quasi-practical test within the operation of theoretical proof itself. The "fideistic" theory that belief is sometimes justified
in the absence of verification is quite distinct
from the pragmatic theory that verification
itself is a practical process. Any theory of

knowledge that corresponds to the realities of human belief must deal with an extensive and all-pervading strain of "overbelief"—of cognitive affirmation that lacks the full warrant which cognition ideally requires. It does not suffice merely to recognize the presence of this strain, or issue warnings against its danger. Since man must live with his limitations, and so far as possible outwit them, a theory of knowledge that is relevant to the actual situation will provide norms to guide belief amidst the semi-darkness and narrow horizons where for better or for worse man is condemned to do his believing. To this question William James devoted his lifelong attention and the resources of his genius. His fideism is his answer.

There are two senses of the term truth—at least two—which it is convenient to distinguish. Assuming that truth is an abstract noun connoting the quality or character which is primarily expressed by the adjective "true," and that this character of being true or false is a character which attaches to beliefs, there are two circles of truth—an outer and an inner circle. The outer or more inclusive circle embraces all justified beliefs. The inner circle consists of those beliefs which possess that restricted sort of justification which it will be convenient to term evidential or theoretical verification. It is the purpose of the present lecture to show, in general accord with the philosophy of James, that the broader or non-evidential justification is *practical*, that is, justification of the type which is employed in order to prove what a man *ought to do*.

In expounding the character of truth in the narrower or stricter sense I shall so far as possible avoid those detailed considerations which divide the reigning schools of philosophy. It is generally agreed that beliefs are capable without essential alteration of being expressed in the form of judgments, and that judgments are susceptible of theoretical proof—capable of theoretical truth, and liable to theoretical error—by virtue of their *form*, and by virtue of their *objective reference*. In form, judgments are affirmative or negative, categorical, hypothetical or disjunctive, universal, singular or particular, etc., and in respect of these characters they are governed by such rules as consistency, contradiction, and implication. If I believe anything, then in keeping with these rules, I may, or may not, or must, believe something else. In so far as the belief obeys these rules it is formally, that is, logically, mathematically or syntactically,

correct; and in so far as it breaks these rules
it is formally incorrect, or commits, as we say,
an error of reasoning. In order to accept this
type of theoretical justification or disproof,
it is not necessary to decide whether the rules
in question are universal and self-evident principles, or the archetypal procedures of an absolute mind, or mere human conventions de-
riving their ultimate warrant from theoretical
verification of the second type, which turns
on the character of objective reference. Judgments have objective reference in so far as
they embody expectations of experience. They
submit themselves to some appropriate and
decisive moment of fact-finding. They are
"about" something, and it is a part of their
intent that when that something is immediately given its deliverance shall be accepted
as the final determination of their truth or
falsity. If they are to be verifiable they must
somehow contain within themselves an adequate location of that sense of shock which
will be taken as their disproof, or that sense of
fulfillment which will be taken as their confirmation. If the shock or fulfillment is unob-
tainable, then the judgments must at least in-
dicate the conditions under which such shock
or fulfillment *would* be relevant.

In short, beliefs are convertible into judgments, and these are capable of two evidential tests, a formal test and an objective or empirical test.

We have next to note that beliefs, as acts of affirmation or states of commitment, can be produced by non-evidential causes. Present belief can be an echo of past belief, my belief an echo of yours—and the power of these forces of tradition and suggestion will be proportional to the "prestige" of their source. Belief once established tends to be stabilized by the force of habit or by the influence of the group upon the individual. Beliefs tend to be implanted in minds which find them congenial or aesthetically agreeable. Finally, men tend to believe what they want to believe, and the clash of opinions often tends not to mutual correction, but to a stubborn partisanship for the belief with which one has identified one's interest or self-esteem. Although the present age prides itself on the discovery of these and similar unreasoning sources of belief, that discovery was already old when Joseph Glanvill announced it in the middle of the seventeenth century:

So that to give the sum of all, most of the contests of the litigious world pretending for *Truth*, are but the bandyings of one mans *affections* against anothers: in which, though their reasons may be foil'd, yet their *Passions* lose no ground, but rather improve by the *Antiperistasis* of an opposition.[2]

The emphasis on this subjectivity of belief has led in the present age to extreme conclusions. Some contend that the powerful and widespread operation of these non-evidential causes so far obscures the light of evidence that genuine knowledge, that is, evidential belief, is impossible. Defeatists of this category are called sceptics. Others accepting the preponderant influence of non-evidential causes, abandon the evidential standard altogether, and reckon as true whatever beliefs suit the subjectivity of an age, a nation, a race, or an individual. These are the historical relativists. Especially interesting and characteristic of the present epoch are the propagandists. In proportion as the causes of belief are disclosed their control becomes possible. Propaganda, in the vulgar sense, is the art by which belief is induced by the use of prestige, emotional excitement, or appeal to practical interest. The present age not only understands these causes, but by a rapidly advancing technology of communication knows how to bring them into

2. Joseph Glanvill, *The Vanity of Dogmatizing,* reproduced from the edition of 1661 (Columbia University Press, 1931), p. 135.

play. In the light of the successful practice
of the art of propaganda it is clear that
belief can be implanted willfully,—by dicta-
tors, preachers, orators, teachers, parents, or
friends. It can be implanted in others and it
can be implanted in oneself; for one can, if
one wills, expose oneself to suggestion or al-
low one's emotional and practical bias to control one's creed.

This being the case, belief becomes a question of conduct. Shall I or shall I not induce
in others or in myself beliefs which do not
have full evidential warrant? This is a practical question, to be answered in the last analysis in moral terms.

If one is *not* to employ or submit to non-
evidential causes of belief, then there must
be a second choice. Evidential belief must be
stated as an alternative mode of conduct to be
preferred, if non-evidential belief is to be rejected. It is clear that over and above the
theoretical justification of belief there is here
implied a *practical maxim* to the effect that I
*ought to promote only beliefs that are theo-
retically justified*, that is, beliefs that are formally correct and empirically verified. Now
it is the practical or moral character of this
underlying obligation which the proponents
of strict science have neglected and which

James, among others, has taken such pains to stress.

During the Renaissance and Enlightenment the champions of reason, such as Descartes and Spinoza, realized that the fundamental issue was a practical issue between the ethics of intellectualism and the ethics of supernaturalism. During the nineteenth century the feud between religion and science was at bottom a conflict between an authoritarian ethics and an ethics of social utility. This conflict was implicitly assumed, but it was rarely understood by the conflicting parties that the principles by which the moral issue was to be settled were not the same as the principles employed by each party within its proper domain. Least of all was this issue to be settled by mathematics or by laboratory experimentation, so that by a curious paradox it was the party of science, sworn foe of dogma, which was, as respects the fundamental issue, the more dogmatic of the two. It is extremely difficult to persuade the scientist, trained as he is to accept the compulsions of mathematics and of experimentation, to see that the *right* of these compulsions to exclusive control over belief is not itself to be established by such compulsions.

The age of propaganda is arousing the

scientist from his dogmatic slumbers. At a sitting of the International Physiological Congress held at Moscow in 1935, Professor Walter B. Cannon seized the opportunity, before proceeding to "technical affairs," to comment on the dangers with which science is confronted in an age of dictatorships and exacerbated nationalism. He raised two basic questions: "What is the social value of the physiologist or of the biochemist? What conditions promote and what hinder his best uses to society?" Neither of these is a physiological or biochemical question. In answering the first, Professor Cannon assumed the position of a utilitarian moralist, and spoke of "the common purpose which binds . . . together" the scientists of "different lands and races, and the vital role which" they "play in bringing benefits to" their "fellow men." He assumed, in short, that underlying his technical procedures there was a moral obligation on the part of the scientist to benefit his fellow men universally and to improve their physical and mental condition. In answering his second question, he emphasized the need of security, freedom of inquiry, leisure, and international coöperation. He affirmed, in short, "the pervasive and universal value of truth-seeking" and of the methods by which this seeking might be promoted and its results universally disseminated.[3]

In this eloquent and courageous address Professor Cannon explicitly recognized, though he did not argue, the ethical premises by which the cult of science is justified. But that cult as a whole is weakened by its failure to invoke philosophical allies against the well-calculated, if meretricious, ideologies of its opponents, over whose minds the mere name of "science" casts no spell.

It is clear, then, that the inculcation of belief by the employment of its non-evidential causes, on the one hand, and the scrupulous restriction of belief within the limits of evidential proof, on the other, are *practical* alternatives. A choice must be made because the two alternatives are in some degree incompatible. This does not mean that they are mutually exclusive throughout their extent, but that there are points of conflict where precedence must be given to one or the other. If the choice between them is to be justified, it is necessary to invoke such reasons as are relevant to practical choice—in other words,

3. "Some Implications of the Evidence for Chemical Transmission of Nerve Impulses," *Proceedings of the Fifteenth International Physiological Congress* (Leningrad, Moscow, 1935), pp. 4–11.

moral reasons. Let us consider what some of these reasons are.

It is a commonplace that the operation of the non-evidential causes of belief tends to weaken the reasoning faculty and to obscure the data of sense. The admission of the forces of habit, suggestion, and emotion reduces the relative weight of evidence, so that instead of being the preponderating factor it may become a mere apologetic or "rationalizing" accessory which gives to non-evidential belief a specious appearance of theoretical rigor. A belief arrived at from non-evidential motives is likely to be adhered to from the motives of pride and loyalty. The mind closed to evidence is closed to correction and deaf to criticism. The early Christians were known among the intelligentsia of their day by their inflexible obstinacy. Charles Peirce in a paper on "The Method of Tenacity" has pointed out the effect of faith on the *will* of the adherents.[4] They "*won't* listen to reason." When the non-evidential causes of belief assume a social form they intrude upon the privacy of the individual mind, which is the only region in which the strict theoretical linkages of inference and verification can occur. Where they assume the

4. "Illustrations of the Logic of Science," *Popular Science Monthly*, XII (1877–78), 8.

form of authority they destroy or starve the
organized agencies of science; they intimidate
the investigator, substituting fear for curiosity or criticism; they prevent the dissemina-
tion of theoretical truth, once it is attained;
they substitute the public forces of prestige
and solidarity for the still small voices of reason and observation.

At this point, then, it is proper to ask, more
proper than the proponents of science are accustomed to admit, "What of it?" If infidelity
to theoretical evidence is a sin against the
Holy Ghost, then it is proper to demand the
credentials of that august sanction. It is now
untimely, if indeed it was ever safe, to assume
that such fidelity is an authoritative and supreme commandment. It is openly challenged
as it has never been challenged since the Age
of Faith.

There are three moral grounds on which
the priority of theoretical evidence in the control of belief can be argued.

In the first place, the activity of the intellect itself, in its pursuit of theoretic truth,
may be assigned a place of eminent dignity in
the moral hierarchy. The scientist who, dis-
missing considerations of utility, considers
truth as an end in itself and serves it for its
own sake, takes this ground; though he or-

dinarily fails to see that the proof of a truth, no matter how rigorous, in itself constitutes no evidence whatsoever of its dignity. Where shall one look for such evidence?

It may be argued that the intellect is man's supreme faculty, and that its autonomous exercise is the "highest" of human activities, realizing the intent of his being, and bringing him the most profound and durable satisfaction. This claim is, I think, doubtful. It derives its chief weight from a lingering Aristotelian tradition which may now be successfully challenged both by the science of man, and by the general experience of happiness. Or it may be argued that theoretical activity is independent of external conditions and is therefore a safe refuge when these conditions are adverse or precarious. The man who finds his happiness in thought or contemplation is independent and free since he has the necessary resources within himself. This argument, too, is of doubtful cogency. It implies the sacrifice of the natural and worldly goods which form the greater part of life; and it neglects the fact that intellectual detachment is a privilege, conditioned not only by capacity and education but by an opportunity of leisure which is created by an economic system of which others must bear the cost. There is, however, another and surer moral basis for the cult of intellect. The life of free inquiry and of contemplation tends to unite men rather than to divide them. Men are brought into innocent and coöperative relations by their theoretical objectivity, while by their emotional and practical subjectivity they are impelled to enmity and mutual destruction. Theoretical evidence is common, and the cult of theoretical truth is non-competitive, since it makes no exclusive use either of its instruments or of its ends. This will be the case in proportion as the pursuit of truth is single-minded, that is, in proportion as it is purged of emotional and practical bias and confined to the strictly theoretic procedures of reasoning, observation, and contemplation. The intellectual activities, thus purified, rank with aesthetic and artistic activities as forms of life which are intrinsically harmonious, and require no moral reconstruction in order to form parts of the good life.

While theoretic activity is non-competitive in its inherent nature, it also serves, in the second place, as an occasion of common action and feeling. Those who pursue theoretical truth, do so, as we say, "disinterestedly." This term, in spite of its negative form, signifies a common passion and a coöperative undertaking. Scientists and philosophers in so far as they are actuated solely by a regard for formal or experimental evidence love the same truth, pool their resources, and rejoice in one another's success. In times of angry partisanship and destructive conflict they keep alive and embody in their own international community the ideal of universal concord. In proportion as their theoretic activity is pure and rigorous they speak a common language of mathematics and experimental technique. Whereas human subjectivity is relatively incommunicable, by their theoretical objectivities the devotees of science and philosophy enjoy a common heritage of meanings and a world-wide mutual understanding. What is true of the theoretic activity in itself is true of the practical enterprises which it promotes. In order that men shall act together there must be a fund of common beliefs. In order that they may agree in practice they must agree in ideas. Common undertakings are as broadly inclusive as the creeds of their participants. A consistency of personal belief is the condition of undivided personality; classes, nations, and races derive a practical solidarity from the convictions which are shared by their members. In proportion as beliefs are dictated by non-evidential causes they tend to the creation of limited solidarities, internally unified, externally conflicting. Purely theoretical beliefs, on the other hand, tend to the creation of a universal solidarity. They form the necessary basis of agreement for all-inclusive and humane undertakings, such as public health, technological improvement, and the cultural arts.

Finally, there is the appeal to utility or control of the forces of nature. It is widely assumed that this is, in the most fundamental sense, what beliefs are for. There cannot, I think, be any doubt that the degree of control is proportional to the purity of the theoretical motive. The historical evidence is overwhelming. Man's mastery over nature has advanced most rapidly when science has been most free from interference by passion and authority, or when men have been most successful in breaking the bonds of habit and tradition. This argument for the priority of evidential belief rests on two premises. In the first place, it is assumed to be a good thing that nature should be harnessed to human uses, and that the physical man should be enabled to survive and prosper. This is a specific ethical premise, self-evident to modern occidental minds, but challenged as illusory or materialistic by every cult of other-worldliness, supernatural-

ism, asceticism, or pessimism. It is assumed, in
the second place, that general human goods
are better than the private goods of individual persons or limited groups. The control of
nature as such is a general human good sub-
serving every human interest. The cult of
pure theoretic inquiry conceives of man as
pitted against an external environment which
dictates the conditions of his survival and
supplies the instruments of his achievement.
It conceives man *solidly* as sharing both the
dangers and the uses which nature presents.
It is a part of this cult that the products of
theoretic inquiry should form a common fund,
freely accessible to all and bequeathed to pos-
terity.

Professor Lewis has framed as the ethical
fundamentum the maxim that we must not
"trench upon high-plane purposes from low-
plane motives."[5] The assumed priority of evidential over non-evidential belief is an application of this maxim. To believe in accord
with the evidence is to serve a high-plane purpose, which must not be violated by the low-
plane motives of emotional preference or
practical bias. When one examines this high-
plane purpose, it proves to coincide with that

5. C. I. Lewis, *Mind and the World Order* (1929),
p. 267.

liberal or inclusive ethics which has already
been expounded.

It is well to remember, then, that the issue
between the liberties of thought, speech, teaching, and inquiry, advocated by liberal nations,
and the censorships advocated by party, racial, or nationalistic dictatorships, is not to be
settled by a simple appeal to the conscience of
either opponent, or by any self-evident axiom.
It is a profound moral issue, between the inclusive and the exclusive philosophies of life.
There is no point in simply arguing that the
fascist or nazi policy is injurious to science.
It is intended to be. It is a deliberate rejection
of the scientist's moral premise. The *cult* of
science is based on a *creed*, and that creed is
the universalistic, individualistic, progressive,
and pacific ethics, commonly known as liberalism. If this creed is anything more than a historic and transient passion, or a local and
epochal tradition—if it is true, or if it is justified—then it is *ethically* true, or *philosophically* justified.

We are now prepared to see that the same
creed which justifies the cult of evidential belief, and establishes the priority of that cult
in case of conflict, will also in certain cases
justify non-evidential belief. The creed is

broader than the cult, and that cult is not its only implication. To deny this, or to place a prohibition on non-evidential belief, would be to treat the cult as though it were a complete and fundamental creed. To defend such an ethics of intellectual abstinence, one should take a position similar to that of the ancient sceptics, who justified their negation of belief by appeal to the simplification of life. He who reduces his beliefs thereby reduces his commitments. Amidst a world of warring opinions or doubtful enterprises he can take refuge in a mood of doubt, and save himself the trouble and the hazards of any gesture more decisive than a shrug of the shoulders. Modern positivists do not usually take this reasoned ground, but content themselves with a dogmatic negation—as crudely dogmatic in its spirit and method as any primitive taboo.

Assuming that evidential is to be preferred to non-evidential belief whenever the two are in conflict, what positive reasons can be adduced for non-evidential belief in the absence of such conflict?

In the first place, non-evidential belief is justified when it is a condition of, or accessory to, evidential belief. Thus faith is sometimes a means of obtaining evidence. One finds what one looks for, and one looks for what one believes can be found. To find evidence it is necessary to believe in advance that the evidence is there; to find reasons it is necessary to believe in the rationality of the world; to seek truth it is necessary to have a faith in truth: all of these attitudes of mind are contrasted with an intellectual defeatism which breeds apathy and impatience. This same attitude of initial belief is necessary in the case of specific theories and hypotheses. If they are to be verified they must be held with a certain tenacity through a period of experimentation. This attitude has, of course, to be combined with a readiness to abandon the hypothesis if after a period of trial the evidence is negative. But this is a question of degree. For a genuine empiricist all beliefs are provisional. So long, on the other hand, as there is any degree of commitment there is some degree of belief. The empiricist will keep an "open" mind, but until his mind is in some degree "made up" he cannot advance at all. Truth is not obtained by a pure receptivity, but by framing and affirming theories which give impetus and direction to the inquiring mind.

In the second place, where the evidence in question is psychological, belief may create the evidence. Belief is an act of mind; as such it produces effects upon mind; and the effect

produced may be the evidence required to verify the belief. To quote James, "the thought
becomes literally father to the fact, as the
wish was father to the thought."[6] This class
of instances is greater than is ordinarily supposed. The most familiar case is the individual's belief in his own powers. The man who
believes that he can win a race, or achieve a
fortune, or win an election, or recover from
illness, or overcome temptation, or renounce
the devil and his works, is, owing to this belief,
the more likely to succeed; provided, of course,
the belief does not lead to a neglect of other
causes. Such inspiriting belief may attribute
the effect to other causes, as when the sick man
recovers owing to his belief in the potency of
a remedy, or the sinful man is saved by his belief in God. One may object in such cases that
it is not the object—the remedy, or God—
that is efficacious, but what is believed about
them. But even were their imputed virtues fic-
titious there would none the less be a strain of
truth in the belief. It is true that the patient
will, as he believes, get well; it is true that the
sinful man will, as he believes, experience a
new life; and these beliefs have made themselves true by producing the evidence of their
truth—always assuming that the belief has not

6. *The Will to Believe* (1898), p. 103.

closed the mind to other conditions of success. The man who puts his trust in God is on that account more likely to prevail, provided he also keeps his powder dry.

But belief has an effect on other minds. If I believe in another person's power or charm, and manifest that belief, as I can scarcely fail to do, that other person's power and charm are magnified, and verify my faith. Broadly speaking, other people are likely to rise to our expectations of them. Those benign individuals who think the best of their fellow men experience the effect of their own radiant esteem. They heighten human capacity all about them. Philanthropy and misanthropy are self-confirming.

These effects are intensified by social solidarity. The blind self-confidence of a group, an army, a party, or a social mass, communicates itself to all its members. The belief of each in himself, and of the aggregate in their aggregate self, may engender an irresistible élan by which this belief, however unwarranted in its inception, produces the effects by which it is justified. All political managers and military chieftains claim the victory in advance, not from sheer fatuousness, nor because they are blind to the obstacles and difficulties, nor from childish boastfulness, but because they understand instinctively that collective self-confidence does in and of itself contribute to victory. The organizers of social movements, whether socialism or fascism, seek to inspire their adherents with a faith in their cause, even when that cause is, other things considered, most precarious. Distrust, on the other hand, is a serious and often fatal weakness. This weakness tends to assail movements such as liberalism in which the critical faculties are most highly developed, and in which emotion and the sheer drive of the will are correspondingly disparaged. The same holds true of the party of righteousness at large, however this be conceived. To believe that the good can prevail, and, so help them God, will prevail, would create in its protagonists an increment of force that might determine the outcome of the moral struggle.

Equally familiar, pervasive and important is the fact that even beliefs which are based on evidence are for the most part based on borrowed evidence. It is only the investigator himself, within the narrow field of his own investigation, and in the comparatively rare moments when he is engaged in investigation, that can be said to "possess" the evidence for his beliefs. The overwhelmingly greater part of human belief is based on testimony and authority. The man who attempted to limit his belief to such judgments as were confirmed by his own experience would be in effect a sceptic, for even in his own inquiries an investigator is dependent for confirmation on the existing fund of established truths. But to accept testimony or authority is to trust the reliability of others. Nor can it be said that this reliability is itself theoretically tested. Even the most rigorous scientists accept one another's reports on general grounds of reputation. As for the great mass of mankind the bulk of their beliefs are *to them* entirely unwarranted. They do not see, they do not understand, the theoretical reasons for their judgment.

In these three ways, at least, then—in the faith which finds evidence, in the faith which creates evidence, and in the faith which borrows evidence—non-evidential belief is an adjunct of evidential belief. Such faith, since it is a means of obtaining certified knowledge, is justified by the same argument as certified knowledge itself.

We have now to consider the justification of non-evidential belief in its own terms, or where it cannot be said to serve as a means to the attainment or extension of evidential belief. There are two cases in point, the case in which the evidence is absent, and the case in which the evidence, though available, is inconclusive.

In both cases the nature of the fundamental argument is the same. If there is no evidence for or against a given belief, then there has been some other and non-theoretical incentive to its adoption. Otherwise the belief would not be there. It commends itself as emotionally agreeable, as auspicious to the will, or as bringing the believer into agreement with himself, with society, or with the past. These considerations can be instantly rejected as irrelevant only provided the obligation to theoretical evidence is assumed at the outset, and is treated as the ultimate premise from which all questions of belief are to be argued. But this obligation to theoretical evidence is, as we have seen, itself argued from ulterior ethical premises, of the liberal-inclusive utilitarian type; and if these ulterior premises are competent to sanction evidential belief, then they are competent to assign it limits and to authorize exceptions. Theoretical rigorism, or the *exclusive* determination of belief by evidence, is only one possible alternative. The real question, then, is not whether non-evidential believing is or is not excluded by theoretical rigorism—of course it is, by definition;

but whether non-evidential believing is excluded by the underlying ethical premises.

Is it harmful to the personal and social development of mankind, conducive to pain, frustration, or conflict, that men should sometimes, in the absence of evidence, believe what for some purely "practical reason" they want to believe? It is agreed that fidelity to theoretical evidence is so important a condition of personal and social good that it should take precedence whenever evidence is available and conclusive. It is true that our readiness to believe without evidence *tends* to weaken the appeal of evidence and to beget habits of theoretical laxity. It follows that fidelity to evidence is a good maxim for general use, and that it is from time to time desirable to harp upon it. Believing for practical rather than for theoretical reasons may even be considered so corrupting a temptation as to be resisted utterly, and it is quite intelligible that those who are obsessed by this danger should promote a cult of total abstinence. But flat prohibitions of this sort are at best secondary rules, designed for weaker minds which cannot be trusted to grasp and wisely administer the first principles from which the rules derive their cogency. The injunction, "Never believe what is not theoretically proved," would, if it

were possible to obey it at all, be a wholesome
corrective for overcredulous minds, not capable of intellectual self-control and nice discrimination; as "Never drink intoxicating
beverages" or "Never tell a lie" are useful for
tipplers or deceivers who cannot safely be left
to the guidance of fundamental hygienic or
social principles.

Let us suppose a belief for which, on the
one hand, there is no evidence; let us suppose
that the absence of evidence is recognized, so
that there is no disloyalty to fact; let us suppose that the believer is scrupulously respect-
ful of evidence where it *is* available, and thus
protected against the formation of a habit of
credulity. Then let us suppose, on the other
hand, that the belief in question fills the believer with hope, makes life seem "worth living," and moves him to morally beneficent action. For the subject in such a situation to
abstain from belief would be quite arbitrary.
There would be no "good reason" for such abstinence. There would be no evil consequence
to weigh against the good. Abstinence would
in this case be precisely as gratuitously destructive as any other form of asceticism. It
would sacrifice the larger personal and social
goods to the narrow satisfaction of intellec-

tual pride or the morbid pleasure of self-mortification.

The same general considerations apply to the case in which there *is* evidence, but in which the available evidence is insufficient. This case arises from the importunity of action. It is *practically* necessary to act before the *theoretical* process is ideally complete, and thus to profit by what evidence there is, however insufficient. The greater part of human action is theoretically premature. The individual must choose his occupation before the vocational experts have perfected the science of human aptitude, and without any complete evidence of future circumstance or development. The sick man must employ *some* remedy before the science of medicine is ideally complete. Men must erect some state, employ some economic policy, adopt some social program when the social sciences are notoriously inconclusive. Action cannot be postponed to await the leisurely completion of the theoretical processes. It is for this reason that inquiry and action are set apart, the one being assigned to universities, to laboratories of research, or to the scholar's study, while the latter is embodied in practical institutions; so that inquiry may proceed without interrup-

tion while action profits by the partial results
already obtained. It is for this reason that
men of thought and men of action disparage
one another, thought being judged doctri-
naire and irrelevant by action, and action being judged loose and dogmatic by thought.
The two are inevitably divided by a difference
of tempo. Each, on the other hand, needs the
other: the investigator depends for the practical conditions of his life and work on the
premature decisions of the man of affairs;
while the man of affairs depends, for what
dim light he has, on the autonomy of the investigator who proceeds in his own way and
takes his own time.

There is, as James expressed it, a "forced
option."[7] The occasion of action will not wait.
It is pervaded by a strain of urgency. All
practical questions contain a factor of time—
it is necessary to say "yes" or "no" when the
clock strikes. Supposing that the clock strikes,
as it usually does, before the evidence is conclusive, it is necessary to adopt one or the other
alternative and accept it as the premise of action. But to accept it as the premise of action is
to believe, with the inevitable consequence that,
having turned one's back on the prospective
evidence, and changed one's mood from in-

7. *The Will to Believe*, etc. (1898), p. 3.

quiry to assumption, one's belief will acquire a growing subjective certitude. This access of certitude under the pressure of action measures the margin of belief over evidence, or the extent to which non-evidential causes have been allowed to operate.

The justification of the practical man's over-belief appears from a consideration of the alternative. Not to say "yes" is often tantamount to saying "no," and the negative answer may be even less supported by evidence. Or, not to say "yes" may mean that one closes one's eyes to the evidence altogether and yields to some other impulsive force. Or, not to say "yes" may mean that the state of doubt is protracted until the occasion of action has passed, and any good which the action might have produced is forfeited. Under the circumstances in which man is placed, and owing to the limits of his faculties and experience, his only choice is either to profit by what evidence there is, and by acting translate legitimate theoretical doubt into some degree of illegitimate certitude; or ignore evidence altogether; or through theoretical scrupulosity lapse into a condition of practical impotence. But the last alternative is possible only parasitically. Speculative doubt is a luxury conditioned by public policy. To take the detached and lei-

surely course of pure inquiry, with its prohibition on premature action, is possible only in
a society where affairs are conducted by less
inhibited men.

There can be no doubt of the choice which
is implied by the premise of liberalism. The
maximum of human satisfaction, of personal
integrity and realization, of social justice and
benevolence, requires that belief shall be bold
and decisive—exposed to the hazard of error,
but avoiding the certain failure of irresolu-
tion. The art of life, in the basic and all-enveloping sense, is to direct activity by the dim
light of half-knowledge toward a goal which
lies beyond the horizon of certain prediction.

Although a contemporary observer might
stress the application of these considerations
to social, economic, or political beliefs, William James was especially interested in their
application to religion. Religious belief may
be a condition of obtaining religious evidence,
as when the presence and saving power of
God are experienced in consequence of an initial and as-yet-unjustified act of faith. Religious belief, taken as a confident allegiance
to God's cause of righteousness in the world
at large, may create its own evidence through
enhancing the morale of its adherents. The

religious belief of lesser men profits by the mystical insight and by the testimony of the spiritually gifted. Religious belief transcends experience. It is the most far-reaching of all beliefs, and is proportionally incapable of such verification as would satisfy the strict requirements of theory. It deals with "first things" and "last things" and "all things." It is the attempt of finite man to live in the light of a hypothetical omniscience. There is, in religion, therefore, at one and the same time, a need for belief beyond evidence, and an unlikelihood of violating evidence. There is no conclusive theoretical evidence against God, freedom, or immortality, and there are strong practical reasons in their favor. Taken together they provide the creed which is most congenial to the emotions and will.

But the basic dogmas of religion are not wholly without evidence. The theoretical evidence is not in itself decisive—religion is not, James "in sad sincerity" concludes, theoretically demonstrable.[8] There is, however, evidence in its favor. This evidence James compiles, appealing to experience in the broad sense, and rejecting that narrower or positivistic version of experience which already presupposes a naturalistic world-order. For

8. *The Varieties of Religious Experience* (1902), p. 455.

freedom there is the evidence afforded by the element of chance which pervades nature, or the deviations of experience from every conceptual definiteness; and the evidence afforded by the immediate experience of the will. For God there is the evidence afforded by the exceptional "energies of men," when they seem, by the lowering of the normal threshold, to receive an unnatural access of power by the tapping of some greater "reservoir." For immortality there is the evidence afforded by the relation of mind and body, in which the role of the body seems to be that of a channel of transmission rather than that of a conditioning cause.[9] In other words, James sought to make religious faith plausible or even probable, and to rid it of all violent conflict with experience.

This being done, the rest is faith. The issue cannot be escaped by prolonging metaphysical doubts. Man's opportunity of profiting by religion is limited in years. He is face to face with the universe and must map out a course of action in which his mind *makes the best* of its imperfect light and limited vision. And he must do it now or never. If he says "no" to re-

9. Cf. James, "The Energies of Men," *Memories and Studies* (1912), pp. 229–264; cf. also above, chap. I, n. 12; Perry, *op. cit.*, II, pp. 373–374.

ligion, that is tantamount to saying "yes" to irreligion. He must enroll himself with the one belief or the other. And if he be to the utmost of his ability a doer of good, in the liberal and inclusive sense, he will be a believer, willing to risk a theoretical error for the sake of a good which if it *were* realized would be the greatest of all goods.

James was by nature a believer. One of his less discerning critics has cast doubt on his genuineness of conviction. "He did not really believe," writes Santayana; "he merely believed in the right of believing that you might be right if you believed."[10] But such a criticism rests on the hasty assumption that it is impossible both to believe and at the same time to be tolerant and open-minded. It is precisely this possibility, difficult and improbable as it is, which James realized. I owe to my colleague, Professor Whitehead, a comparison which at least in its application to James seems to me more penetrating than Santayana's witticism. John Dewey, he said, is, like Calvin Coolidge, essentially a Vermonter who hesitates to "let himself in,"—his philosophy is a tentativism, designed to avoid any final plunge; but James's philosophy is expressly

10. *Character and Opinion in the United States* (1920), p. 77.

designed to justify and embody an attitude of
self-commitment. James did, it is true, feel
that "your robust and full-bodied faiths
. . . begin to cut each other's throats too
soon," so that "refinements and reasonable-
nesses and moderations have to creep in."[11]
But this tone of magnanimity and standing
offer of reconcilation did not weaken the force
of his belief.

Who shall say that it is not humanly possible both to believe, and also to harbor saving doubts; both to cast in your lot with one
party, and also respect your opponents; both
to feel a passionate devotion to your own
cause and yet desire to give every cause a
hearing; both to believe yourself right, and
yet acknowledge the possibility that you may
be wrong?

In this brief exposition of ideas which are, I
feel, congenial to the philosophic spirit of
William James, I have not attempted to con-
ceal a certain strain of incoherence. This is
not because I have wished to employ the rhe-
torical trick of paradox, tempting as that is.
Nor is it because I have wished to charge
James with inconsistency. There is inconsistency, no doubt. It would be strange if so hos-

11. Perry, *op. cit.*, II, 237.

pitable a mind, profoundly pluralistic both in temperament and in doctrine, had not harbored ideas that were irrelevant or even contradictory. I have been told that in playful dispute with Howison at the time of the great California earthquake James appealed to that catastrophic tremor as evidence of what he called his "loose-jointed universe." It would have been surprising, or too loose-jointed to be credible, if a philosopher who felt himself, and liked to feel himself, the inhabitant of a loose-jointed universe was not somewhat loose-jointed in his thinking.

But I have hoped to suggest something beyond this. I have hoped to suggest that James achieved, both in his thought and in his personal character, the sort of spiritual statesmanship of which only great minds and great philosophies are capable. Their greatness lies not in their strictness, but in their inclusiveness. They do not ignore. Ideas which, if taken in isolation and pursued obliviously of other ideas, assume a character of harsh repulsion, are through the mediation of genial minds enabled to live together in mutually fructifying peace. Traits which in lesser men we are accustomed to deem incompatible, and are grateful to find distributively, are here disclosed as complementary perfections.

Such men are miracles of magnanimity—hints of what it means to be an integral thinker and a complete man. It is in this sense that I would speak of James's metaphysics as presenting a pluralistic universe, incurably plural in the existence, meaning, and values of its components, and yet by virtue of a connectedness of next with next, and a general interaccessibility of region with region—a genuine universe; of his theory of knowledge as a fideistic empiricism, exalting immediate experience as the source and prototype of all theoretic achievement, and at the same time recognizing that beliefs derive their ultimate warrant from the purposes that govern the will—praising science for its empirical restraint, while also providing wings for the flights of speculative metaphysics. It is in this sense that I would present James himself as one who was both loyal and cosmopolitan, a man of taste and yet promiscuous in his human relations, a human and highly socialized lover of solitude, a tender and peace-loving militant—a man of ardent convictions who was nevertheless modest in his claims and open in mind both to opposite opinion and to the ceaseless battery of novel events.

INDEX